The Definition of True Beauty;

Beautiful Who, Beautiful Me, Beautiful You.

By

Kara Reed

Preface

We live in a world that embraces diversity and change, while at the same time excludes certain individuals and groups based upon those differences. This book is dedicated to all of the women and girls, like myself who have never felt beautiful and always felt worthless.

Growing up, I not only was aware of my physical features that I hated, but as I grew older I realized that I was not the only female struggling with body image. For those that struggle with low self-esteem, negative body image, depression, anxiety, and fear I stand with you.

I too have been where you are and I only want to shed light from my perspective and definition of what true beauty is and encourage you to embrace your beauty and know your worth. Lastly, I dedicate this book to my beautiful Grandmother Doris L. Reed, pictured below who passed away July 6, 2016 and my mother on the cover holding me as a baby. These are the two women that I first saw as beautiful in my life.

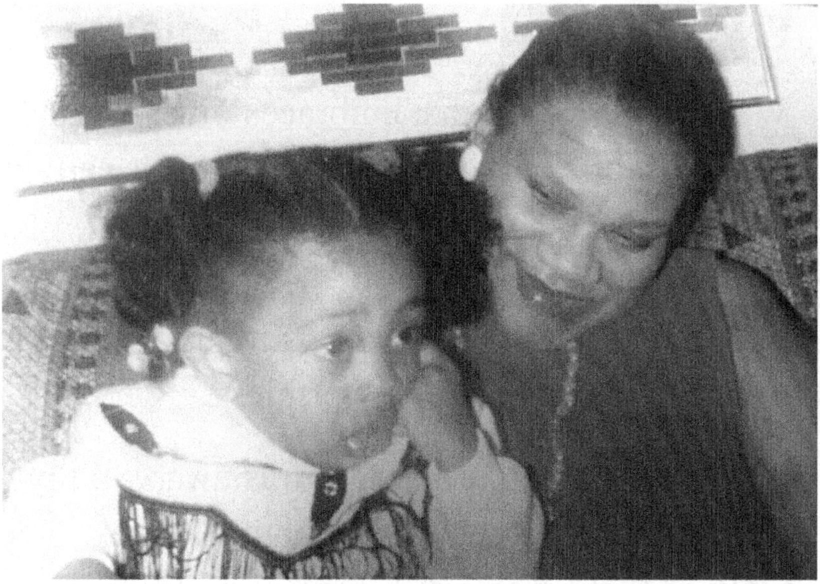

Table of Contents

Preface

Chapter 1: Boxed Beauty...........................1

Chapter 2: Ugly......................................20

Chapter 3: Media...................................50

Chapter 4: Materials..............................86

Chapter 5: Men 106

Chapter 6: Beauty Hurts: Comparing and Competing...181

Chapter 7: What is Your Beauty Worth?..205

Chapter 8: Reborn Beauty....................220

Sources..274

Chapter 1

Boxed Beauty

I began thinking to myself what does it mean to be truly beautiful, and how does one define beauty? A beauty that is beyond physical, something that is more than our physical attributes. So, I began to do my research on various websites and beauty was defined as a simple characteristic. In America, a woman is exalted or crucially judged based upon her beauty as opposed to a man. In this country alone, there are hundreds of pageants for women and girls to sign up for. Pageants, conventions, and modeling competitions in which officials and the world judges a woman solely upon her body.

It is no surprise that America and the world is obsessed with thin, white or light skin, long hair, and Eurocentric physical features. As this type of beauty has been repeated through media and other forums. Today the past standards of beauty still exist with a bit broader examples of exotic features, super thin build, or perfect coke bottled shaped women. In our world, I often hear and see individuals commenting on which female is "exotic versus average." People like me do not fall into these "exotic or beautiful" categories and are usually left out of Americas definition of beauty. In such a melting pot of a world, America still directly and indirectly promotes thin, white, light, or fair skinned, blonde hair blue eyed "Barbies" as the superior beauty.

As a young girl I had a fun and wild imagination that consisted of me talking as well as acting out characters in my mind. Almost all of my Barbie dolls were white, I thought they were all beautiful, but why didn't I look like any of them? I was a lanky black girl with thick glasses, acne, and I always believed I was the ugliest in my class. I remember in 6th and 7th grade, my classes were filled with dark, brown, and light faces. I remember one day the boys and girls in my 6th grade class talking and ranking the girls, from which were the prettiest to the ugliest.

The girl that was rated prettiest was the only biracial girl, with light skin and long black curly hair. I along with a friend were called the ugliest, I was a silent mouse but I heard everything said about me. However, as I got older I wondered why weren't we all rated the most beautiful girls? I too used to wear my towel on my head pretending I had long flowing hair as my Barbie dolls had. Seems since the beginning of time, the female body has always been placed on display as an object.

There is so much pressure placed upon a woman to do it all and have it all together at the same time. Today, there is so much pressure to lose weight, dieting campaigns, dieting pills, and many other forms. But is the message of truly living a healthy lifestyle no matter what size you are being equally stressed to our young girls and women?

Men are also placed upon this pedestal in which their bodies are sexually objectified on a certain level. However, this level does not seem to be equal at all when it comes to the female body, which seems to be more sexually objectified. Growing up I would see constant images of the female body on television, magazines, and billboards. From certain advertisements to music videos that always showed women dancing around in provocative clothes.

So, my question is why has the definitions and roles remained the same for so long? It seems as if men can get away with being unattractive, bald, missing teeth, overweight, and still be considered the hottest man in America. I was bullied extremely in the 6th and 7th grade, I internalized being called weird, ugly, retarded, slow, and mean things because I was a shy and quiet girl. I know that kids can be cruel and brutally honest. So, as I internalized the pain, I began believing that being ugly was my fate. Every-where I looked I saw pageant girls, videos, advertisements, magazine covers of white, or light skin being glorified.

I wondered, if I had thick glasses, long black tightly coiled hair or what my peers teased as being nappy headed…how I could possibly be considered beautiful. The westernized standard of beauty has been so heavily engrained in our minds, that it is hard to break. The westernized idea of beauty is a Eurocentric standard of beauty. After doing a bit of research and seeing the documentary called Hue, I realized that this westernized standard of beauty was global. There are girls struggling with body image and low self-esteem all across the globe from India to Nigeria, and countries that some have never heard of.

This Eurocentric standard of beauty is seen as thin, long blonde hair, and light colored eyes; from straight hair to straight noses. Implementing that if one possesses these features, then she represents the superior beauty over all others. I also watched the dark girl documentary and saw the struggles that women with dark skin face on a daily basis, I cried watching this documentary because I could relate to some of these women experiences, which were similar to the Hue documentary.

To some people I am brown skinned, to other cultures I have dark skin. I view my skin as black skin, beautiful black skin. As a black woman I have felt inferior and ugly because of my skin color and facial features that were non-European. To women and girls in India, Africa, and all over the world that are being taught to hate their dark skin. You have to know that your beautifully colored skin, a colored skin of all shades is beautiful.

To those same women and girls with lighter, fair, or albino skin, your skin too is equally beautiful. As children we are raised to believe this is a false notion, and that we are all equal. I learned through school that light or white was pure, good, and represented cleanliness. When I was younger I thought that white or light beauty was superior, as that is all I was used to seeing getting the most attention. I just longed to be beautiful like the Barbie dolls that I played with. I wondered why the models in the Cosmo and Ebony magazines were so pretty with perfect skin and European facial features. I scrolled down my search findings of beauty and saw it was defined as the qualities that give great pleasure, or satisfaction to see, hear, or think about. (Dictionary.com) In American history we see the definitions of beauty constantly evolving, yet staying within its same box.

The stories of pin up girls, 1950s pageants, and myths about the female body. It is nothing new that women continue to be judged upon by many factors, such as their womanhood, physical beauty, grace, how good of a mother one is, or how she carriers herself. Besides my own experiences, through one of my sociology classes I took my freshman year, I began to understand how marginalized women and girls are. The history of beauty pageants date all the way back to 1835, in which women and girls are being judged upon their physical appearance. In a country such as America with a history of oppression, discrimination, racism, sexism, and abuse towards its women. Every day I look around and see that our girls are becoming very lost in our society, because I too was once one of those lost girls.

I believe some of them need a sense of direction, however this direction has gotten lost over the core years. Women having been objectified from bathing suits to being told how to dress, hair, and overall physical appearance. Women also being oppressed, from voting to not being allowed to obtain certain jobs as men. Back then women did not have equal rights as men, and it is still a daily fight today for us to be paid equally for our labor in the work place.

The jobs of housewife, home maker, baker, and stay at home mom were the full-time jobs, but not anymore. The womans job was to remain beautiful even while getting dirty and a full-time job like the husband was out of the question in the 50s. The woman was nothing but a trophy, which was to stay in the case and never leave its BOX. As

American culture and media is controlled by majority forces that have the money and power to control what we see. The womans body has many different physical features that media chooses to decipher through their ways of manipulation. The people we see in advertisements are women.

There is an unfair balance of what the definition and roles are considered for men and women. So, I wonder what is beauty, the science of beauty, and why are young girls targeted at such young ages to look according to this in your face standard of beauty they are surrounded by. The definition of beauty tends to have come from a majority rules culture which is westernized America.

The history of beauty is changing as technology improves and connects us with the world around us. There is obviously something in our brains that allow us to be attracted to one another. The physical features have become so crucially important that many women are quickly weeded out of the boxed definition of beauty. The female body is placed upon a pedestal and it is to be maintained according to Americas definition of beauty. It seems as if limits are constantly placed on a woman's ability, as a way to continue to control us altogether.

There is still a sense of dominance and power that men want to continue to obtain in our society. See, I planned to spend an entire chapter on the history and science of beauty. However, as I used the internet and people around me as sources, I found out almost every definition relating to beauty was related to ones physical appearance. As well as the science of what one is attracted to physically. The world we live in preaches do not judge a book by its cover, yet we all do every single day. The daily judging, stereotyping, prejudices, or preferences can often lead to discrimination based upon ones appearance. In my opinion we are all of the human race, so why does physical appearance matter so much?

Beauty is constantly being re invented and edited each year. As to whose average, basic, beautiful, exotic, or this ideal superior beauty. Whether people choose to acknowledge that women and girls are pressured to look according to this standard boxed definition of beauty. Beauty is constantly challenged every day and often girls are trying to change their appearance as young as six years old. Girls at early ages are taught to be graceful and just look pretty. We are constantly obsessing over how a woman looks based upon her physical features. In the world, we are all born completely different, yet so much emphasis is placed upon the right features, or good looks a female has.

To the point of where parents are able to pre-select the physical features of a child they want before he or she is even born. The history and science of a womans beauty has gone on for a long time all over the world. I think the true science of ones beauty is not based upon physical appearance and is defined by God. In my opinion he created all of us, therefore making us perfect in his image period. I plan to declare that and make it known throughout this entire book.

Chapter 2

Ugly?!

This chapter is dedicated to whom America deems as the ugly, and not so physically attractive. I was one of those people for a very long time and I always thought of myself as an extremely ugly person. On the inside I was a happy girl growing up, until I began to get older and realized that everything was based upon ones appearance.

The sadness began around age 11 and I remember being called ugly, four eyed, nappy headed, big headed, to that weird quiet girl. I was often an outcast and chose last simply based upon my looks and timid personality. I was never popular and I remember being called ugly so many times that I became immune to hearing the word. From 6th and 7th grade being bullied so badly, I began to believe and internalize every evil word said about me.

I know what it is like to sit in an overcrowded classroom from public school to private school and sitting in an overcrowded classroom with peers that make fun of you on a daily basis. As I had my head down in 6th grade I remember the two girls around me talking about how my underwear was dirty, because it was showing, and how my khaki pants were flooding, as my ankles showed. I remember I looking up at the substitute teacher who said nothing and did nothing when I was being made fun of, same applied to a few of my past teachers who turned a deaf ear and blind eye to the bullying I endured. I never felt beautiful or pretty, especially when I was called so many terrible names.

My mother raised me to treat everyone with respect and compassion, I was always a good girl, and I did not know how to defend myself. I stuck to making fun of myself and remaining silent as my only defense mechanisms. In 7th grade it was time to line up for the bus and it was me and a few of the other kids still in the classroom. As I was the first person to line up at the door, the rest of the students played around in the class and moved slowly to line up, the teacher commented "why can't everyone get in line on time like Kara." Then one boy smacked his lips and yelled, "that's because she's a nerd!" the remainder of the students all began laughing.

As I turned around I saw the teacher make a weird uncomfortable smirk at the boy, yet said nothing, that was one of those days I got off the bus, headed home and cried before doing any homework. The bus was no better, a lonely bus ride home, kids kicking the back of my seat, and making fun of my hair and once again my flooded khaki pants. To the time when I transferred from Cleveland public school district to Warrensville, then back to a Cleveland private school, that my mom could barely afford, even with my voucher.

During my time at that awful private school in 6th and 7th grade where I endured the worst bullying and I accepted being called ugly and retarded and this is the place where my self-esteem drastically went downhill. The bullying I endured was a very traumatic experience for me, as the impact of negative words began to shape my identity. The effects of bullying I endured began to shape my identity without me even realizing it. Then when we moved to the suburb of Shaker Heights, I was new and shy and the 8th grade was one of the loneliest years of my life.

I had no friends and I remember sitting in science class and a girl walked over to her friend who sat across from me and said "how can she be a nerd when she is not even smart," then the boy sitting next to her looked directly at me, and responded to her comment, "it's because she is a lame." I pretended as if I heard nothing, just because I was quiet did not mean I was deaf to the insults I endured from my peers. To this day I remember their exact names and faces. It was as if I started to believe something was mentally wrong with me, every time my class mates called me retarded. This was the same class I remember a girl from the tennis team, walked past me and said, "why is her head so big" and began laughing as she past.

To another girl who sat by me in class and called me weird just for looking her direction. I absolutely dreaded picture day in high school, because I remember lining up for the individual pictures and being stared at and laughed at by two of my peers. I remember the name of the biracial boy who called me fish face during biology class and hearing laughs, to the black girl who sat behind me in Algebra and talked about my hair and how bad my split ends were. There was also the time I was in 9th grade art class and I had my head down, because that day was awful.

I remember the art teacher telling me to pick my head up or leave her class, instead of possibly asking me what was wrong, she called my mother, I was right there listening to her ask my mother if I had a learning disability. Sadly, we often mistake those that are quiet or introverts for being unintelligent. Then in one of my favorite classes,

English Literature taught by Mr. Harley, I overheard a girl saying that I sounded like a man and how weird I talked in high school. To another girl who always said I looked lost and asked me did I have any friends and did I know anyone in the class, in a condescending tone, trying to make fun of me for not really knowing anyone.

To being in one of my favorite classes, which was ceramics taught by another amazing teacher by the name of Miss Weiner, who believed my pottery creations were good. On the first day of ceramics, I sat across from another girl, she stared at me for about 10 minutes, then got up and said, "ugh she's weird" and moved to another table. I also remember being at my locker during my freshman year of high school, I was switching out text books. As I heard 3 upper classmen girls a few lockers down the hall laughing and saying, "who is this ugly girl with the big head" and as I walked past them, one female said "ugh" and they began laughing as I hurried past them to my next class.

    I grew immune to hearing "ugh, ugly, weird, and laughs as I walked past any one. To the health class I was in and the bi racial girl I sat behind, said "she is so weird" to another male classmate sitting next to her and his response was "who?" She said, "the girl behind me." For all the times I was called weird in high school, today as an adult I embrace being weird, I embrace being a beautiful weirdo, a beautiful anomaly. To young girls, it is okay to be shy or quiet, just never stop being yourself.

During my time in high school I had about 3-5 friends off and on, but I always felt so alone, by the grace of God I made it through those four years. I had my happy times and moments in high school, but I disliked high school because this is the one place I saw some girls being the most vicious towards one another, not really physically, but most of all verbally. I thought to myself one day the tears would end, yet even in my adulthood I found myself still crying the tears I cried in 9th grade. When I ran cross country for a semester in high school, I did so terribly I remember hearing one of the girls say how she "felt so bad for me" because I was struggling to keep up with the other runners.

All of those words hurt and further contributed to me hating myself even more, I hated my inner and outer. I never received the proper help with my low self-esteem, depression, and social anxiety before entering college. I remember meeting my first roommate in our quad during my freshman year at Indiana Tech and being so withdrawn that when she was trying to talk to me I was quiet and giving one-word answers, from there we definitely no longer spoke. To the time when I transferred to Ohio State University and instead of engaging, I isolated myself out of fear of rejection and anxiety from being bullied in the past.

I once went on a make a difference day trip by myself and I isolated myself, because my depression, anxiety, and fears had consumed me and I completely shut down. I was also hurting from the past, so I came off as quiet, rude, and standoffish, all while silently suffering. There were parts of undergrad that I enjoyed, but I really needed help. Therefore, I struggled immensely socially, emotionally, and academically. As I was used to rejection and isolation. I became a mean and cold person towards many people that entered my life, I was always on guard when it came to mean girls.

Sadly, I still believed every negative word my former peers said about me in high school and elementary school. I was still carrying around this baggage and I'd look in my dorm room mirror and feel so inadequate. All I saw was my acne, wide nose, big head, uneven skin tone, big lips that looked purple, my mustache, and I hated my

African features, I hated the fact that I looked like my Liberian father. I wanted my mothers light skin and I wanted a straight nose, I wanted to look like the pretty popular girls on campus. The ones I saw getting most of the attention from males, and the ones in the television ads.

I also think back to my junior year of undergrad in math 116, and as a transfer student I did not know anyone at Cleveland State University. This was a crowded class and coming directly from one of my other classes, I remember never getting to sit exactly where I wanted to, because so many people were already there as soon as the class doors opened. So, I had always sat one row over from this girl that always made mean faces at me, and this particular day, she turned back around to her friend and said "She has the weirdest looking face ever." Her friend looked back at me with a weird smirk and that day I went home, cried, and wrote my heart out in my journal.

    I am glad that day happened, because it fueled me to pick back up my pen and began writing this book in between classes, as I finished up my undergraduate degree. I first started writing when I was nine years old, poetry and stories. My pencil was my voice, as a shy quiet girl. I will never forget the names and faces of all the people who called me ugly, retarded, and weird, to the ones that laughed and said nothing. Sometimes you never forget who the bullies were and the friends of the bullies. When you laugh at the joke or remain silent, you are doing just as much damage. I will never forget feeling like such an outsider throughout elementary and high school.

Then I thought I cannot believe I am still letting these words pierce through me, the same words; ugly, stupid, retarded, and weird. I always felt I was never good at anything, I would always get decent or bad grades throughout grade school, so I believed I was dumb. Sure, enough as the bullying got worse, my grades would go from decent to worse. I cried and prayed to God for years, asking why am I so ugly, Lord please make me prettier! I remember asking God to make me smarter, and anything to simply "fit in."

I grew up in a diverse world, but I still didn't see women on television that had my wide nose, acne, full lips, glasses, or thick hair. I saw this repetitive definition of beauty in movies, music, pageants, and everywhere else. The pretty or main girl was usually white, light, long straight hair, flawless skin, and super thin. The prettiest girl was always being chosen first, whether it be homecoming queen or cheerleader, the prettiest girl was always very popular. One thing is for sure, you cannot run from your issues, as soon as I graduated from high school, I wanted to get out of Cleveland and run far away from the people and places that hurt me. There is no running, you have to be brave enough to face your issues head on.

I was always a shy tomboy at heart, which is why I never understood how much emphasis was placed upon a womans physical appearance until I got older. It saddens me that the world in which I am growing up in is losing its true values and morals in many respects. What ever happen to the idea of all people being created equally, thus forth everyone is beautiful and unique in their own way. I remember very vivid details of being bullied about my appearance, from how I talked, looked, and even walked.

    I struggled with my appearance from dieting, trying to look super thin like the supermodels, and trying to gain weight to look thick like the video models. Once, I almost considered plastic surgery all just to feel beautiful, I was about 19 years old and I wanted to change my nose, get implants in my breasts and butt just to look and feel beautiful.

At 21 years old I read a lot of books and magazines, in which I did not see women that were representative of my appearance. In America, when it comes to beauty, there are the haves and the have nots, and I have grown very tired of being one of beautys have nots. Self-esteem is something I always battled with as a little girl and stems into my life as I write these words as a part of my healing.

I learned quickly that my glasses, thick hair, and acne were not acceptable. I began to learn these definitions of beauty by watching and listening closely to the world around me. According to the world, beauty is Eurocentric, thin, competitive, jealous, and women can either praise or tear another woman down based off her physical appearance. Why are women so vicious and harsh towards one another? Is there a such thing as the most beautiful woman or girl in the world? My answer to this question is yes, and toward the end of the chapter I will discuss why and who is.

Another reason that I started blogging was to spread the love of God and how he has worked in my life, and be a light of encouragement to women and girls battling the same issues as myself. In January of 2015 I began blogging under the name of Flawed Beyond Perfection (now Cherished Beautiful Creations), when I came up with this title I realized that we are all flawed human beings. None of us are born perfect, therefore we are flawed beyond our make-believe perfections, thus forth flawed beyond perfection.

These so-called perfections may be makeup, high heels, implants, hair extensions, or anything else we deem as flawless. For example, many women often use the term to describe how flawless ones hair or skin is. It is nice to compliment and uplift one another by using the term flawless as a term of endearment. However, there is no such thing as flawless, because we are all one hundred percent flawed beyond our false perfections. Once you realize you are flawed beyond your so-called perfections, you will understand that you are a cherished beautiful creation, created by God.

There is this unattainable notion of perfection that exists in our society that must come to an end. It is okay to be flawed and beautiful, the flaws are a part of who you are. For example, another of my flaws besides acne is the black birthmark on the back of my right leg. I had a very long list of things that I hated about my physical appearance, I allowed my flaws to define who I was. I wanted to shrink the size of my head and scrape all of the acne off of my face, and magically make my birthmark as well as stretchmarks disappear. I disliked the sound of my voice, heck I just wanted to be pretty enough for people to like me. Do not believe that you are ugly or were born ugly, your flaws are beautiful and so are you.

For so many years I allowed everyone else to define my beauty, because I did not know what true beauty was until I got older. I grew up hearing the phrase "they think I'm pretty so I must be pretty." This is a common problem because we cannot give other people the power over our beauty and worth.

I remember when I got into my first relationship during my senior year of high school and at 17 years old I was thinking I hope his mother, friends, and family think I am pretty enough and good enough.

    Sadly, I was always worried about being pretty enough for other people, pretty enough to meet his parents, pretty enough to marry and have his children, prettier than his exes, and am I pretty enough to keep his attention. These were all the wrong questions and wrong thoughts that I attached to my physical appearance, because I based my worth on my physical appearance. Instead of walking in my true beauty, I was too busy trying to live up to societies standard of beauty. This is what happens when you become so heavily concerned with other peoples opinions of you. I am fed up with Americas direct and indirect meaning of beauty. As our girls and fellow sisters continue to be sexually exploited, trafficked, raped, and abused.

All the while there is far too much importance being placed upon the female body and how sexy or glamorous it must be at all times. The female body has been on display for centuries as a trophy that must remain shiny 24/7. I just began to write the words, Am I not beautiful, *Am I not beautiful because of my dark skin and thick coiled natural hair, am I not beautiful because of my hijab, am I not beautiful because of my wide nose and light skin, Am I not beautiful because of my freckles and full figured curves, Am I not beautiful because of my thin figure and shoulder length hair, Am I not beautiful because of my bald head, or long hair, Am I not beautiful because of my full lips and cornrows, Am I not beautiful because I use a wheelchair, Am I not beautiful because I am blind, Am I not beautiful because I wear sneakers instead of heels, Am I not beautiful because of my acne and stretchmarks, Am I not beautiful because of the burn scares that cover my body? Am I not beautiful? Who made you the judge of beauty, if I am not beautiful then please tell me who is?* There are so many factors behind why girls and women, like myself never feel beautiful. I am not blaming anyone or anything, but my mission is to redefine beauty from within, not from without.

After considering all the factors that affected me personally, I came up with the 3 M's. In which each M stands for a factor, Media, Materials, and lastly Men. These are three consistent factors in which women and girls let define, determine, and set the standard for THEIR beauty. As I write this book in between classes, I began to understand what being beautiful truly means. To answer the earlier question, there is no such thing as the most beautiful girl in the world, because WE ARE ALL EQUALLY BEAUTIFUL.

Chapter 3

Media

Every time I turn on my television, read a magazine, see a billboard, or listen to the radio I would feel ugly and a sense of inferiority. Scrolling through Instagram photos of women and girls with captioned photos of "no filter" definitely did not help.

    Because like everyone else I was comparing my flaws to what I saw as their perfections and wanting to look as glamorous as they did. As I began this journey of reclaiming my self-confidence, I knew I had to rid myself of the media outlets. Whether it was a weekly or yearly long fast from television to social networking sites. I needed a break from the constant arguments, bashing, and competing over which girls picture received the most "likes." The images on television screens constantly use the female body for objectification for almost any product.

Then as I turn on the television, I observe adult women behaving like little children, from fighting to basically everything else. The beauty pageants, reality shows, fashion runways, sitcoms, videos, movies, consistently showcase this boxed definition of beauty. Which is thin shaped, coke bottled shaped, or thick video model shaped woman. So where do girls fit into this box, if we, the average women and girls are constantly excluded. Along in this box, is hair which is best if long, straight, loose coiled, weaves or tamed non-threatening hair.

These factors are so crucially important, as some employers do not want tight coiled hair or what some called nappy hair, braids, locks, or an image that is deemed threatening or nonwestern. I have read many articles in which women were terminated based on the style of their nonwestern hair styles, such as braids or locks to women in the entertainment field that may be too dark or not light enough for a specific job, role, or advertisement. Which is vice versa, when one may see an open call for only minorities or a specific group, for serving a specific purpose.

This is understandable, but our society has to be more inclusive in taking a stand that all beauty is equal beauty. We give media so much power by watching and daily engaging in all the forms of media, and most people do not even realize it. The constant advertisements from skin toning, skin lightening, weight loss, acne cream, and so many other products. In a world that teaches me to be myself and love the skin I'm in. Well it sure doesn't seem that way, surrounded by millions of advertisements and retouched magazine photos. Media often uses their boxed definition of beauty as its standard and leaves people like me feeling inferior to this definition.

What if I loved my acne and thick tightly coiled hair, because it's only a part of my physical beauty, my true radiance is from within. Many women and people will disagree with my definition of beauty.

As the movement of non-slut shaming continues by many celebrities, models, strippers, and everyday women who enjoy being naked publicly. I do not agree with slut shaming, nor do I agree with any form of shaming whether it be education or anything else. I have felt the effects of education shaming, as soon as I graduated with my Bachelor of Arts in Black Studies, I got the terrible responses of "oh what made you choose that or good luck finding a job face."

As women we have the right to do what we please with our bodies, minus acts that are considered illegal in America, such as prostitution. I too wear what I want and love dressing fly, but not for the attention of others. I wrote this book to encourage girls and women to find empowerment not solely in their physical appearance, but finding empowerment by understanding your beauty is from within and that is where your true beauty lies. There is nothing wrong with feeling sexy or beautiful when you are naked or reveling skin. Whether you are sending selfies to the one you love or just posing in front of the camera, it is awesome to embrace and love your body period.

Do not get caught up in false validation and confirmation from individuals about your physical appearance. However, I believe slut shaming and embracing being a slut or whore definition is further promoting a lifestyle of promiscuity for girls and women to follow, and promotes a mentality of "since men can sleep around then so can I" which is true, but unfortunately men will continue to be praised, while women are not.

    Yes, men can be naked and not shamed, while women will forever be ridiculed and shamed for doing the same thing. I have been called a slut, hoe, b*tch, and everything else and those words hurt deeply. Yes, the double standard will continue, as a man may be praised for releasing a nude selfie, as opposed to a woman who will automatically be shamed. Although some women and girls receive popularity and praise for sleeping around and simply not apologizing for being called a slut or whore, nor apologizing for their behavior. There is nothing wrong with owning your sexuality and being proud of who you are, but our society will not always be receptive.

I remember teachers encouraging us to dream big and reminding us that we could be professors, sports players, musicians, artists, engineers, inventors, and so much more. Some fields legal or illegal may pay a lot of money, but the cost is not worth your soul, your integrity, your dignity, and all the things that make up your good character. I am writing these words to remind women and girls in America, you can be whatever it is you want to be, just be prepared to work hard for it and never stop. To those women and girls that have the choice to be anything you want, the choice is yours at the end of the day, I only encourage you to discover your true beauty.

You do not have to sacrifice your self-worth and sell your body in order to start your business or sell the next bestselling novel. Usually, in the play area of childcare centers or classrooms, there is a dress up section. Where you see children playing dress up, they are pretending to be doctors, police officers, to princesses and princes. Whether the child is holding a briefcase or stethoscope, children take pride in who they are pretending to be, they take pride within their wild imaginations. I was a child with such a large imagination, my imagination took me places that I dreamed of going to as a child. My imaginations took me places outside of impoverished Cleveland.

I played with my barbies and toys with such joy and fulfillment. As I got older I realized my imaginations can easily turn into reality, and those imaginations can become fulfilled dreams and goals. You do not have to get impregnated by a wealthy man in order to become successful. Nor do you have to get body enhancements to be beautiful. You do not have to allow a man to be your entire means of financial, educational, or any form of YOUR success. Once you figure out your passion, pursue it with all your might, and fight for it. I tell myself every day that no matter how hard this gets, I am not going down without a fight.

I am fighting to pursue my passion so that I can finally live in the purpose and destiny God has placed on my life. I am fighting for my future family, fighting to one day be debt free, and able to stand on my own two feet. Fighting to help my mom pay off her bills, and fighting to attain my piece of the American dream. What are you fighting for, keep it in mind and keep fighting! Yes, there are going to be a lot of No's and obstacles along the way, but as the cliché goes, all you need is one yes, so keep fighting.

If you want to start that shoe line, go to school and major in business, fashion design, do whatever it takes and get it done! Keep your grades high and work your butt off to receive full scholarships and whatever you do keep working. Whether you are working towards a GED or your fourth Ph.D., keep going! Be open to making meaningful connections professionally and personally. Work your way up towards success without compromising your dignity, self-respect, and self-worth. Look in the mirror and ask yourself, do I want to become successful without selling my body or doing something that goes against my morals, all for that promotion or raise.

Do I want popularity and fame, for the cost of my reputation, morals, self-worth, integrity, and dignity? Once you realize you are priceless, you will understand that selling your body for a 1 million dollar check or billion dollars will never be worth it, because you must know the power that lies within your self-worth and true beauty. Also ask yourself what is the legacy that I want to leave behind, can I change, and how can I be a role model to the people I encounter on a daily basis. Are you leaving behind a legacy of millions of nude selfies, narcissistic snapchats, and Instagram posts that scream "me, me, me, look at me?"

Is your time consumed glued to your phone comparing and competing with other women, attacking your boyfriends baby mother, planning to expose screenshots and pictures, and the list of social media messiness continues. Take time and think about how you are spending your precious time. If I could go back and not have sent pictures of my body to males that only wanted to use me and my body, I would have, but I will discuss more of that later on. How have you paid it forward and what will people remember about you and your service to the world.

Unfortunately, using and manipulating men for a child support check, as well as getting implants in your butt and breasts for the most likes and financial gain is becoming very popular. Which is another reason why I wrote this book to encourage girls and women to not be deceived by the images on your timeline, or on television. It is easy to take your clothes off and pay for body enhancements, then later call yourself a masterpiece or legend. I am sorry you are wrong. Finishing school when they said you would never be nothing, now that is a masterpiece, creating something from nothing, using your brain to execute your skills, now that is a masterpiece.

Being a leader instead of following the crowd makes your actions legendary, your character, dignity, skills, and how you apply them towards making a difference in this world is creating a masterpiece. You define who you are and you are the boss, so be exactly that. No matter how much money you make, your reputation, and starting foundation can sometimes overshadow your current accomplishments. Many people praise and glorify women that are proud to be famous for being naked, famous by association, or any other claim to fame, that many judge as talentless.

I believe we all have talent and skills, created by God. I am not judging women who are in these professions or started there, as God is the ultimate judge of us all. However, with this book my goal is to encourage women and girls to value their true beauty as sacred. I do not believe in encouraging our girls to grow up to be sex workers or the next booty model dating the hottest entertainer just to remain relevant aka popular and famous by associations. Do not allow yourself to be a puppet or robot and continue to be fooled. As the old saying goes, everything that glitters is not gold.

As I read about women trying to get pregnant by a wealthy man and having miscarriages all to be pregnant by someone with fame and money. It saddens me to see and read about the lengths and risks women are putting their bodies through all for a little fame, money, and attention. It saddens me to see girls dying from butt injections, complications from waist trainers, and breast implants. But anything to be the baddest or coldest female. Do not be fooled by the lies, because sleeping around and not using protection, may leave you with unwanted pregnancies, diseases, and a long list of soul ties.

If your only life goals are getting VIP in the hottest clubs and sleeping with as many A List celebrities as possible, then you really need to reevaluate yourself. My heart goes out to these type of women and girls, who have yet to discover their worth and true beauty. There is so much more to life than being wrapped up in someone elses identity and someone elses definition of who and what you are supposed to be. I challenge you to be exactly who God called you to be. Media places the pedestal in the hands of celebrities, models, actors, people on television, or those with money.

So, in order to be beautiful, I have to be on the cover of GQ, people magazine, vogue, or the latest womens magazine. Little girls like me grow up thinking they would never make the cover of 100 most beautiful people list. Media also places the myth in our brain that if we look like one of the models or celebrities, or obtain exotic features, then we are automatically beautiful. I remember feeling beautiful when people said I looked like a particular singer or celebrity. I never felt beautiful looking like myself. The last time I truly felt beautiful was in May of 2009, the day I went to prom. I remember getting my nails done by my sisters friend, and another one of my sisters friends coming to do my makeup, while everyone waited outside and in front of the house to take pictures.

I was so nervous after putting on my dress and looking in the mirror, I was shaking as my family cheered when I came out of my room and began taking pictures, I was so happy. This particular day I felt like I was a beautiful princess and deep in my heart and mind, I actually knew it this time. As a child I loved playing with Barbie dolls, because with my huge imagination, I was always the prettiest doll with long shiny golden hair. In order to be beautiful does a girl have to look like a piece of plastic or be dressed as if she is attending a fancy ceremony? Our society is teaching our girls that being promiscuous, narcissistic, and jealous, are seen as beautiful traits.

As we constantly see women fighting, competing, and tearing one another down verbally. This behavior is applauded and often rewarded to certain individuals. The media will forever glorify the nude female body, but not just any naked body. It must be completely perfect and photo shopped to the very tee. This naked body that is always glorified from cleavage in any area to completely naked. The common scantily clad bodies I see are usually thin or coke bottled curves.

In movies, the prettiest girl showing the most cleavage is desired and respected by her peers. In this stereotype the typical pretty girl is not the smartest, yet her looks are compensated over her brains. Media is glorifying beauty over brains, but why can't both be equally important in our society? The more skin a woman shows, the more her body is praised if she fits medias definition of beauty. Media has its way of daily brainwashing us by depicting whose beautiful and who is not. Technology does not help, when so many websites are filled with hate, through social media, articles, blogs, forums that negatively target the female body.

The female body image is constantly being praised and attacked by media. I refuse to let media and other peoples ignorance tell me if I am beautiful or not. As we see many women and celebrities taking a stand against their bodies being edited and photo shopped. Media expresses how to keep up with the Joneses, and how to stay in style by constantly consuming things we may not need at all. Social media is further adding to girls and women feeling insecure about the way they look and feel about themselves. I remember I was in college, when I saw on television and websites, people ridiculing Gabby Douglass about her hair, I thought this beautiful talented girl just made history at the Olympics! Yet we had so many individuals within our society focused solely on her appearance. This is a sad reality that media continues to perpetuate and program its definition and standard of beauty through so many outlets. Have you ever asked yourself why you are taking hundreds of selfies, only to further edit and add filters before posting the photo to your page. I remember when I first started taking selfies in high school with my older sisters digital camera and uploading them on Myspace.

I was posing in ways that I saw other girls posing, just trying to look cute and get attention, all while still feeling inferior. How many selfies are you posting, with hashtags that say "baddest b, flawless, I woke up like this", yet you still feel ugly. Physically I was smiling in all of my pictures, while my heart and mind were miserable and in pain. I was suffering from low self-esteem and I acted out my insecurities through social media, like so many of us do today. As I look at my social media today in January of 2016, things are only getting worse.

As I see and hear girls and women bashing one another from head to toe. I began to wonder why do we bash women for dressing conservatively, bashing a girl who has vitiligo, bashing a woman for remaining a virgin, to bashing women for not losing their baby weight fast enough. As if she has to lose weight period, berating some while praising others, we must really check ourselves. It is one thing to be humorous and make jokes, which I myself have done. However, being a mean girl appears to be getting worse. When I am on social media and I see certain comments it brings me back to elementary and high school days.

I remember being in class and a girl sitting behind me saying to her friend "what is this, the lion king" as she referred to my big curly afro. When I ran cross country for a semester, I remember sitting, waiting in the hall of the gym as the other girls around me stretched, as we waited for the coach. A girl from the volleyball or softball team said, "what is this ugly girl staring at, I'm about to go punch her in the face" and a girl standing next to her laughed. I quickly looked away and thought of ways to defend myself if she were to walk over to me, man I so wanted to sock her in the face that day.

I honestly had many days I grew tired of people making fun of my appearance, my voice, and simply making fun of things I could not change. Being called weird and ugly so many times took a drastic toll on my self-esteem. I could not help that when I was bullied extremely in the 6th and 7th grade and from there I struggled with being an introvert. During a frat house party I went to my freshman year of college, I walked past a girl who played on the basketball team and as I passed her, she said I looked dirty. Now at 24 years old, I still remember the names of the girls who made fun of my hair.

That day my hair was pulled back in a braid and one girl pulled on it then walked away and said it looked like a fat turd. That was when I was in the 7th grade at Holy Name Elementary school in Cleveland, Ohio. There were so many times I was called a bum, because I did not have the labels or name brand clothing as my peers had in elementary school. Then I remember being in 11th grade government class at Shaker Heights high school and a girl sitting behind me, saying "why is her head so big" and the boy sitting next to me looks over at me and starts laughing.

This is the same class another boy sitting on the other side, a row over from me, turned around to his friend and said, "yeah her skin tone is bad." I once again sat there and pretended that I did not hear any of those comments. My weapon was ignoring, putting my head down, or going to the bathroom to escape. But there is no escaping vicious words from peers or anyone. My healing led me to forgive, but those days of verbal torment and tears hitting my homework sheets, and the nights I cried as a kid, it felt like never ending tears. You have the power to take control of your beauty and it starts with your mind. Social media brings me back to those days, of being called bum, ugly, big headed, and nappy headed so many times that I lost count.

Being a shy person suffering from low self-esteem, people did not understand me, especially being 19 years old and a freshman in college, back then I didn't understand myself. I remember an old friend showing me how a former roommate commented under a Facebook picture I was in and referred to me as being "mute." This was not the first time I experienced this, as another girl in high school once referred to me as being invisible. I remember her joking and saying, "She is like one of those invisible people." I never realized how other peoples words were impacting my life.

    These are just some of the hurtful words that I internalized and allowed to define me. Whether it be a joke or not, words hurt period. When I started writing poems and short stories at 9 years old, my pencil was my only voice. I also now realize I hid behind books and writing, because these were my two escapes. I allowed bullies and mean words to silence me my entire life, I did not know how make friends or build healthy relationships or be beautiful internally, I based my beauty on my outer appearance. Writing not only gave me a voice, but it gave me hope and from there, God began showing me that I had a purpose in this world. The things we truly need for survival, seem pretty simple, however media says we must compete with the popular girls, the pretty girls, and the one percent in order to seem or stay relevant. Which leads me into my next chapter of the second M, which is materials.

Chapter 4

Materials

The materials that we consume every single day from shoes to clothes. Whether it be from a certain product that one may be better than the other, as opposed to a non-name brand. The materials of hair weave to fake eye lashes, skin cream, and everything else that media says will extenuate ones beauty.

These materials are always changing and growing within different markets. These materials we use to enhance our physical attributes can be very costly. The material items range from zero to billions being spent on items we may only use once or twice. However, some people do not calculate the total cost of their hair weaves, high heels, makeup, designer bags, tanning, and whatever else. In order to keep up with celebrities, or fit into medias standard of beauty, women will do whatever it takes no matter the cost.

    From women to the youngest of girls are consumed in the materialistic culture we live in. Am I not pretty because I don't have long hair, and I refuse to conform to wearing a 22-inch Brazilian, Malaysian, or Peruvian weave daily just to fit in. Beauty is more than what we buy to conceal our imperfections that God created. God will always be almighty and perfect, but it seems now that if women could purchase perfection, they would surely buy it off the shelves. I was taught not to judge a book by its cover, but our society is telling us materials define ones being and socioeconomic status.

Our society often judges women solely on their appearances, so if she is dressed in a certain manner she might not be taken seriously at all. However, I guess this can apply to all people. I often observe the women I interact with daily, from complete strangers to family. I notice how physically looking good can make you feel good, but that isn't always true for some women like myself. Despite not having friends entering high school, I gravitated towards people that looked like me and I just sat with people that looked like they would be my friend or accept me, like minded introverts or other misfits I guess.

I remember going to the school office to obtain my first work permit so that I could make some money to buy my own clothes. After starting my first job at 15 working as a courtesy clerk at The Fresh Market, I helped my mom with bills and spent extra money on many things. My older sister introduced me to makeup, when I went to my first high school homecoming. After switching from glasses to clear contact lenses and looking in the mirror wearing makeup for the first time, I loved it. I remember going to the mall and buying my first MAC powder foundation.

At this time I struggled immensely with my confidence and having low self-esteem. I began to hide not only my acne, but my identity behind layers of makeup. This was one material I let define my physical beauty, because if I did not have it on, I no longer felt attractive. Lipstick, make up, shoes, handbags, and all other necessities are cool, but who are you as a female underneath all of those materialistic items? I struggled my entire teenage years thinking certain clothes or hair styles would automatically make me more beautiful.

To my surprise I was absolutely wrong, the high heels, new hairstyles, and make up, yet I still felt ugly. I grew up around the culture of my peers who wore designer labels and would do anything to obtain the newest and latest fashions. The ones who always wore designer labels and expensive looking clothing, were the cool and popular people in school. However, I came from a single parent household in which my mother made less than

20,000 dollars a year, so me and my sister did not wear any designer labeled clothing. If it was designer labeled, best believe it came from the GW aka goodwill.

I remember my mother always taking us to thrift stores and affordable department stores. We live in a materialistic society that thrives off and encourages consumers to keep consuming no matter if you are poor or wealthy. So it is okay to be late on rent, as long as you look super pretty for Saturday nights party? Living outside of ones means is a whole different story that I do not plan to tackle today. My whole argument is for women and girls to understand that material items do not define who you are. When I hear comments like "This dress makes me look fat" or "This Gucci dress makes me look ten times better" or the common "I look so disgusting" that one may hear in the female fitting rooms.

You do not look fat or disgusting in these materialistic items. Even if one looks great, one has to know they are beautiful from within, in order to understand it is not the clothes that make you who you are. I just feel we are all going to have our days of ups and downs as women, when it comes to body image. But my goal as a young woman is to encourage more women and girls to have more beauty ups than beauty downs. The materials we are surrounded by can drive one crazy if she lets it. I always ask the question of did I buy these shoes to impress my friends or did I buy them to go with a specific outfit, or did I buy these shoes to feel beautiful?

I dated my second ex who liked girls with light colored eyes, and I remember one time I ordered hazel colored contact lenses online so he would think I was prettier. I never told this person I brought them online, and wasted my money on something I only wore once. As soon as I put them in my eyes, I looked in the mirror and no longer saw Kara. After 5 minutes of staring in the mirror, all I saw was the fake hazel lenses overshadowing my large dark brown eyes. Did I mention those went in the trash the same day, I was once again fed up with trying to fit into someone else's definition of beauty.

I came to the realization over time that low cut tops, tight fitting clothes, and make up is not what made me beautiful. I struggled with what I saw in the mirror every single day. To this day I still struggle looking at my face without the foundation, eye shadow, and eyeliner. I wore make up every day in high school to try and hide my acne as well as my insecurities. For years I let the concealer conceal my true identity and beauty, as I moved out of my tomboy phase. I slowly began to become a slave to the products my older sister introduced me to. Once I got my first job at 15 years old, I was spending a lot of my money towards material items, from getting my nails done every other weekend, hair straightened, and buying more make up just to feel beautiful.

I always wanted to look pretty like the popular girls in my high school, Victoria secret angels, cover girls, and the girls I saw in the beauty pageants. Until I finally came to the realization that those women and girls do not set the standard for what beauty is. We as women and girls have the power to re define the definition of beauty and set our own definitions, not according to the world.

Another material can be using substances like alcohol or drugs to feel better about yourself, this usually is a temporary high or fix. I remember during my undergrad years I mainly drank alcohol to fit in and numb the pain I was feeling. However, nothing helped me, but prayer and constantly crying out to God. The materials we consume are surely addicting, yet we must determine the balance. The balance of not letting our material possessions define who we are as women and girls. I now know that I am a selfless good friend, intelligent, loving daughter, humble, hard worker, and God-fearing individual. However, all throughout high school I let material products and beauty products define my existence. Can you think of any material items in which you over indulge in on a daily basis?

There are so many items that we possess in this world, in which many of them are items that we do not need. As we all know the needs versus wants can be completely different in terms of survival. For example, one does not need implants, make up, or the latest designer labels to survive. Although some women feel as if they need these items to even exist in our world. Often our society outcasts those that cannot keep up with the Joneses and encourages name brands and designer labels, as opposed to thrift stores.

Growing up in poverty, I remember getting made fun of because my shoes and clothes were never name brands. Even in a school where we all wore uniform, I remember a girl calling me a bum in the 5th grade, we were headed outside for rec time aka recess and she yelled down the steps

"Kara look like a bum." My mother brought us what she could afford and she took us to thrift stores almost every weekend. I learned the value of hard work and money at a very early age. Even at 15 when I received my first job, I continued shopping at thrift stores and department stores.

I was about 15 when I opened my first bank account and my mother taught me lessons of spending, budgeting, and managing my money. I remember when I overdraft my account a few times, she told me "you cannot make purchases when you do not have the funds in your account Kara." My mother explained the minus sign, negative balance, and current balance to me very well that day, along with the overdraft fee that the bank had forgave. My mom sat me down and said, it's okay we are going to go into the bank and ask if they can forgive the charges for this first time. Financial literacy was all so new to me and I was just a teenager, but those money lessons I still value today.

My biggest splurge was often MAC make up products. The first time I had worn makeup was during my 9th grade homecoming dance. When I looked in the mirror, the first time with makeup I felt like a beautiful young woman, no longer a girlish tomboy. The makeup made me feel pretty and very mature at my age. As I began to wear it more, with each brush I was brushing and powdering away my innocence. I went from wearing a full face of makeup at homecoming to wearing it every day to all of my classes. The makeup became my armor and shield to negative words I would hear classmates say about me.

    I would blend my makeup to make it look as natural as possible. All the while feeling ugly and inferior, the makeup made me feel a sense of importance. At this time, this was one material that I could not go a day without. The materials are not crucial for survival in this world, yet our society teaches us that we need certain materials to represent our status. I went to a suburban high school with some girls that had everything, from driving expensive cars to wearing makeup and high heels. I often felt extremely inferior to these girls that I would see walking through the hall ways. Food slowly became an edible material in which I indulged in when I was depressed.

From chocolate milkshakes to large portions of fatty foods that made me feel better as I was eating. I was so full, yet so desperately empty inside. My point of this chapter is to get you all to realize, that material possessions do not have to run your life. If you are not happy with your appearance like I was, do not think materials will all of a sudden make you happy. Do not drown yourself in material possessions, because I realized that these possessions only temporarily satisfied my sorrows. The long-term joy I seek concerning my physical appearance ultimately comes from within.

I always wondered why women cared so much about materials that are supposed to "enhance" our beauty. But what about enhancing our minds, we care so much about materials, but do these materials care about us as women? No, so why do we let materials such as handbags, weaves, heels, makeup, and others define who's beautiful and who's not?

One last question, are you beautiful with or without your material possessions, that you own? Which leads me into the very last, and most important M in NOT being the defining factor of your beauty.

Chapter 5

Men

As we all know, men in our society and all over the world obtain a lot of power. This is the last of the 3 M's that women let define their beauty. We often see this play out in our daily lives, as soon as a boy calls a girl ugly, the young girl like me shuts down emotionally or tries to figure out ways to enhance her beauty. Men and women are often very judgmental of one another when it comes to physical appearance. In society men search for beautiful female trophies to exchange, shelf, and keep on display. Our society gives men the opportunity to harshly criticize and judge a woman solely on her physical appearance. I once came across an article written by a male psychologist and published in a major psychology magazine. This was an article on why black women are considered the most unattractive women in society.

I remember reading this article backed with scientific reasons as to why black women were the least attractive group of women and thinking how ignorant, yet I began to question my wide nose and brown skin as not being worthy of beauty. Could this psychologist be right? So, if I am a part of a group considered the ugliest, then whom were the most attractive group of women? To my knowledge there is no such group or thing! Yet this was someone providing statistics and research studies as evidence to define which women are beautiful. It seems as if men prefer the beer girls, models, video vixens, or any slim, coke bottled figured woman.

This world constantly displays men choosing the busty girls over the brains. I remember the first time I was called ugly and weird looking by a male in school. The words pierced through my flesh and sunk into my mind. Those words never dissolved until I began to define beauty for myself. Men can easily scar an innocent pure mind and heart if the female allows it, and sometimes it happens without her realizing it. When I lost my virginity at 18, I no longer felt beautiful on the inside nor out, this further added to my battle with low self-esteem. I often looked for men to tell me if I was beautiful or not, solely relying on their manipulating words. During my undergrad years of dating I remember having initial conversations with men about their physical preference when it came to women. During these conversations I would compare myself to the girls, in which they said they admired.

Based on their standards, I wished for larger chest and lighter skin, because I did not value my physical appearance. You may not pretty enough for him, his mother, friends, or family, but God created you to be pretty enough. During my freshman year of college I remember a male I had classes with asking me why I looked better in my pictures than I did in person, he said it so quickly and casually that I remember smiling and saying I don't know. I was at work and brushed it off, but that comment stayed in my head.

I internalized that comment long before I met him, because I used to take pictures at different angles just to hide my flaws. When I started using online websites to date, I felt as if I looked better online than I did in person. Online dating was my safe zone, it was easy and comfortable. I was able to hide my acne, and flaws just to be pretty enough for some of the men online. Although I still felt ugly, online dating gave me a bit more confidence. My heart hurt every time I would walk past a group of males and hear laughing or comments about my face, head, or hair.

Like the time I was in high school and leaving out of one of my classes and as we all were exiting, a boy said loudly "She got a dome head" and the students around him all began laughing, those words once again pierced through my skin. People love making fun of my head, especially males, to the one male I dated that would occasionally call me a cone head. There were times when I joked about the size of my own head just to mask the real pain, because as I got older I became even more insecure about not only my head, but my entire physical appearance. There are so many conversations I had with men that left me confused and trying to live according to their standard of beauty, which was often westernized and based upon societies definition.

Every time I talked to a new male I would always ask "what would you rate me on a scale of 1-10?" usually the answer was 5-7, I was used to hearing nothing above 8. I, like other girls and women wanted to be considered a dime or the perfect 10 that society deems as the perfect flawless beauty. I was so naïve and dumb to allow a number to change my entire mood, once again I was giving my power to men and boys. I foolishly used to think there were different levels of beauty, such as fine, cute, pretty, adorable, sexy, beautiful, gorgeous, and words men would use to describe an attractive female.

There is no such thing, these are once again words used to divide women, no matter what he calls you as a term of affection or flattery, you have to know that you are truly beautiful. Just as our society labels many different groups of people in our world to either divide or unite. Everyone has an opinion of whose pretty and who's not, but it is up to you to know that you were born pretty and beautiful. When I traveled often via greyhound to and from school or to see ex's that I met online, I encountered more words. I walked past a guy that looked directly at me and then said to his friend, "she is not cute at all." I was extremely insecure about my stretchmarks on my butt and back of my legs. I hated my body, but pretended to hide my insecurities with makeup, clothes, or anything to make me feel pretty.

From my acne, weird looking toes, to stretchmarks, I allowed men to strip me down as average, basic, and ugly. From age 18-23 I allowed men to validate my beauty and worth, I tried to look this way, do my hair the way his ex did, be thicker than his ex, have light colored eyes like his past ex had. I remember going to Applebee's with an ex and he couldn't stop staring at a female across from the restaurant that night.

I was angry and went home thinking I should have worn something tighter or shorter and maybe that would have kept his attention.

I have so many stories similar to this one that I rather not go into, but long story short I allowed myself to be disrespected in so many ways, age 18-23 were my lost years. I was lost, yet through each trial God was breaking me and teaching me valuable lessons about self-love, and many hard lessons that ultimately led me back to him in 2014,

I found myself trying to continue serial dating and rebound from an ex that broke my heart, but God kept saying no. Every time I tried to date, I was rejected or the person I liked was already taken. After graduating from college May of 2014, I was jobless, lonely, and struggling to figure out how I am going to pay all of these student loans that are coming due in 6 months.

I burned bridges and quit job after job, struggling with anxiety, panic attacks, depression, and low self-esteem. I found a job elsewhere, met a guy online and relocated to Columbus, Ohio the following October. I had only been talking to the guy for a month, but I was lonely and trying to feel the void of an ex. After arriving in Columbus I only stayed 2 weeks, because the guy I was with parents wouldn't let me stay with them, I stayed the remaining days at a motel, and three nights at my old childhood friends apartment.

I cried in that motel, and every time we argued, the short-lived relationship was toxic, and ended when I headed back home. I blame no one but myself for entering into relationships in which God already showed me 100 red flags in the first phone conversation, but I ignored them. Ignoring Gods warning signs, is like not using your rearview, and side view mirrors when you are trying to parallel park during a driving test, if you don't use the mirrors you will hit the cones and ultimately fail the test. That October when I came back home from Columbus, I was jobless, confused, and once again in pain. I gave my body, my time, and everything else and he still did not want me. November of 2014 I was laying in my bed praying and I told myself this will be the last year I ever allow any man to disrespect me and my body.

Since October of 2014 I remained single and focused on God, my family, and finally achieving my dreams and goals. I grew up as that shy black girl with pig tails, acne, and large circular shaped eye glasses, I was teased for things I could not control. I was naturally a shy introverted tomboy, that loved running, playing outside, and making up stories as I played with my teddy bears and Barbies.

Outside of school I knew we were poor, yet my mom worked her butt off to provide us with the best childhood I ever experienced. From playground trips, summer camp, circus visits, fireworks on the grass or at the beach, we were a tight family unit and still are. When I experienced laughing as I walked past a group of girls on my way to class or hear a comment about my nappy hair or the size of my head, my family was always there to make me feel beautiful. My sister found out I was being bullied from my mom and ever since 7th grade, she was like my second protector, my backbone, my voice when I was voiceless. My older sister stuck up for me when people would say "who is that or why is she so quiet," I remember her always re directing or finding a way to change the subject. Val's response would be "she's not quiet, she's just shy or she would challenge me by saying, "She has a name, ask her."

My older sister slowly but surely over the years began to teach me how to use and find my voice. She would tell me to look in the mirror and say "Kara you are beautiful and you are smart."

Before I got help for my anxiety, depression, and low self-esteem, I did not realize my older sister and mom were my very first counselors and teachers. When we were younger, my older sister would take me everywhere with her and she brought me things like clothes to bring me out of my shell. My mom always thought I looked beautiful in any outfit, as long as it wasn't too short or too tight.

There were times I would tell my mom I hated my appearance and I used it as an excuse to not go to certain events. My mom would say, "Kara if only you knew how beautiful you really are." I understand now what she meant, my mom wanted me to see my beauty from the inside and out, she wanted me to see the creative artist she saw, she wanted me to see the vibrant happy girl that loved jumping on the bed, the girl that had so many cavities from eating cotton candy and too much Halloween candy. My mom wanted me to see her baby girl, the beautiful girl she loved with all her heart. During undergrad years, I will never forget the tears I saw in her eyes, when I was leaving to Delaware and New York to see two different exes, men that I met online.

    Despite fear, anxiety, and depression, I traveled and spent my last dollar on men that barely knew my full name, an ex that had two cell phones, one that I had no idea about until I questioned and he got mad at me for asking about his other phone. I was a broke college student all throughout undergrad, yet I spent any bit of extra money on another one of my out of state exes, that basically broke my spirit and worth with his controlling words and demeanor.

This was the same ex that when my mother and sister first met him, my mom said why does he seem so controlling and my sister wanted me to immediately stop dating him. I was only 19 turning 20 and they saw the red flags before I did. During the beginning of my undergrad years, I acted out after my first relationship failed, I did not love myself, I felt ugly and simply worthless. Not only did I disrespect my mothers rules, I was letting her down, because she knew my true beauty and worth long before I did. My darkest moments were in those times that I allowed men to use my body and manipulate my mind, 18-23 years old I was lost on a downward spiral of serial dating, fooling myself into thinking I was in love with each new "boyfriend." As I have said, these men said all the right things that my no confidence and low self-esteem needed to hear.

As I dated male after male, talked to random people online, I felt so lost and my self-esteem and confidence dwindled each time I received negative feedback. I remember being 19 years old almost 20 and feeling like the ugliest female in the world. Every black male that I would date or end up talking to preferred light skin, mixed girls, Hispanic or white girls, and girls that were thick. I use to feel so inferior to what they described as their ideal partner.

I have been called fish face, big nose, retarded looking, to one ex saying that my nose wasn't that bad, in meaning it was not that wide so that helps my attractiveness, makes no sense right? I was foolish and naïve, to think many of these males I was talking to were darker than me, with large and very wide noses, yet the same features on their face that matched mine were inferior through their eyes. It was not until I got older that I realized how insecure, jealous, angry, and manipulative some men really are. My mom and sister were there after every male left my life and disappeared.

I cried when one long distance ex moved on 3 weeks later and posted him and his new gf on Facebook and Instagram. My heart hurt when males left silently out my life and disappeared with no explanation. I use to wonder would sex make him stay, or money, or maybe if I had green eyes and light skin, like the girls he fantasizes about. All the wrong thoughts, and all lies from Satan. From ages 18-23 were the years my tears burned my face, those tears hurt because I felt like my world was over every time someone left or tried to comeback. Do not be a revolving door like I was. During those years I was not only a puppet for men to manipulate and play upon my low self-esteem, but during those years I learned so much about people and myself.

God was breaking me and bringing me closer to him. When wolves tried to enter I would immediately close the door, I began seeing right through smooth talkers and mind games. I began looking at peoples actions, character, heart, mind, and spirit. This is why during your journey of defining your beauty, find the roots in your life, like my mother and sister, those people that are firmly planted and speaking life into you every chance they get. I remember that last ex that moved on in 3 weeks, I allowed to break my heart in January 2014, I was so low that I was graduating with cum laude honors from Cleveland State University, May of 2014 with my bachelor of arts in black studies. Yet, all I could think about was my ex and his new Girlfriend to the point where I did not want to attend my own graduation, because the one person I wanted to attend was not there.

    This is why you have to know your worth, know who you are and embrace your true beauty on a daily basis. It took me a year and some change to get over that last heart break, but with God I was able to move forward and be at peace. I regret all of the pictures and videos I sent to men that did not deserve me nor my body. I regret allowing men to use my body whenever and wherever they wanted, as if I were a disposable piece of trash. Every time I sinned that is exactly how I felt, like trash.

I learned too many lessons to repeat the same mistakes, therefore I vowed to never chase a man or anyone that no longer wanted to be in my life, I vowed to cast my cares on the cross, I vowed to trust God and allow him to use me, and work through me. I will never forget the disgusting feelings I felt after every sexual encounter I had with males that did not care about me. To the time I met up with a past time I had been talking to online, and invited him into my dorm, and after he left I was scrubbing my body and crying in my tiny dorm room shower.

That same night I looked in the mirror and thought in my head what are you doing, this is not you. During these years I hated looking in the mirror, because whenever I did God would convict me even more and when I looked in the mirror, not only did I feel ugly, I felt filthy. So many times I wanted to scrub off my sin and shame. Towards the end of October 2014, I listened to God, and decided I will stay single and celibate for however long you want me to. But after 2 years past, I fell back into my old ways aka sin. Ever since then I have been fighting hard to stay on the right path. Going through many experiences taught me the importance of loving yourself and really taking care of your body.

Take whatever steps you need towards being internally healthy and happy. I have been focused on God, and helping women that have struggled with low self-esteem and never feeling beautiful. I have been trying to become more confident and building my social skills, one step at a time, as I break free from anxiety, depression, low self-esteem, and suicidal thoughts. I will never forget I was headed into the library at CSU towards the end of my junior year and as I was walking past a female janitor towards the elevators, she approached me right before I entered and said "Sweety walk with you head up, you are beautiful." I looked down and said thank you, she had no idea how that comment made my day, heck made my year!

As I began thinking back to why are girls and women so vicious and mean towards one another, I thought back to many of the encounters I had with women, from coworkers to peers all throughout my educational experience. I remember over hearing one female coworker talking to a male coworker about me and saying how I was not cute at all and at the age that I am now, I have grown so used to hearing worse. It always stung more when another female from the same race as me, black just like me, made those comments. No matter what race, gender, class or socio-economic status you come from, it is so important to build up one another and not continue the trend of tearing one another down.

That was also the month I began my journey to getting the old happy Kara back, the happy before 6th grade Kara, and as I begin reading my word, writing, and loving myself, the joy is slowly returning. However, the one thing I always longed for and the void that was never filled, was not having a father. The one male that we are first introduced to as girl is our father. I was one of those girls and daughters that grew up without a father. Growing up without a father or male figure in my life was the only major void that I felt and this also had a lot to do with why I never felt beautiful. If you grew up without a father, absent parent, or have no family then you may understand where I am coming from. It is so important for a female to have a father in her life.

As I got older I did more research by reading studies and watching documentaries. Then I looked at my own life and began to understand that my behavior displayed that of girls that grew up without a father. According to a Psychology Today article, children without a father are more likely to suffer from anxiety, depression, fear, and obtain issues developing healthy relationships.

They also reported that girls who grow up without a father have a higher rate of promiscuity and are prone to be exploited by adult men. As well as being at a greater risk of being a victim of emotional and sexual abuse. Seeing as all that I have done and went through, I fell into this statistical category. I love my mother with all my heart and am grateful for her, but growing up I longed to have a father in my life. My mother would tuck me in at night and tell me that I was beautiful and we would recite the Lords Prayer up until I was 14 years old. Even after that, we always said the Lords prayer at night, my mother taught me about the power of praying and trusting God. However, there were so many times that I wished I had a father to tuck me in at night and tell me that I was beautiful. I wanted a father to protect me, provide for me, and treat me as if I were his princess.

My mom was my superwoman growing up and I always wished I had a superman to be my father. In high school I envied anyone I knew that had a father in their life. I did not realize that I so desperately wanted to have the love of my absent father as a child. I did not know how to love myself, nor did I know how to love another male. When I went through being bullied, I went home crying, wishing that I had a father to protect me from classmates that I feared. My father resided in Canada almost my entire life and currently resides there. I only got to know him through phone conversations and seeing him twice, once when I was 6 years old and another visit when I was about16 years old. We only spoke on the phone about three times a year and every time my heart broke. My heart broke because as I got older, the child living inside of me realized that my father left me with many broken promises. I felt abandoned by my father and his broken promises only threw salt in the wound. When you tell a child that you are coming to their high school graduation and you are coming to America to see them and never show up, it hurts.

For me these broken promises cut deep, because I remember phone conversations with my father at 8, 11, and 14 years old and getting excited, thinking he was coming to visit me and my sister. I remember asking my mother could we go to Canada and my mom saying no because she did not have the money to get all three of us there. After taking a trip to Canada with my sister to see him when I was about 16, I got to see who I looked like and understand him a bit, but it felt as if I were meeting a stranger. Around 18 when I was entering adulthood I no longer cared to obtain a relationship with my absent father, I simply gave up. I figured why should I try to reach out to a man that does not know my birthday, nor calls, yet gets angry and yells at me for not calling him.

    Why should I reach out to a man that barely shows any desire to get to know me as his daughter. To this day my older sister no longer communicates with him either. I have heard his temper many times taken out on my mother, sister, half-brother and myself, mainly through voice mails filled with profanity and yelling. I use to blame my father for not being able to trust men and trust people out of fear that they would abandon me like my father did. I never knew my father, all I knew was an angry man yelling on the phone, all I knew was the man that abandon me at birth.

During college I sought after older men for love, affection, attention, protection, and guidance that I never received from my father. When my first relationship failed I sought to rebound with anyone and everyone to fulfill that void. At 19 I entered a relationship with a man that was 27 years old and after that failed, I was online talking to older guys. This second ex I spoke about earlier was the most toxic, verbally, mentally, and emotionally abusive, he was the one that almost broke me. This was also the one that used me, as I sent him money and paid for everything when I went to see him in another state, all on my broke college student funds.

I pursued older men for validation in every area of my life, especially when it came to my beauty and worth. If I couldn't be my fathers beautiful princess, then I would be some mans princess. Sadly, the little girl inside of me acted and cried out for attention from men, trying to fill a void that only my biological father could fulfill. All of my exes were men that I met online except for my first ex, and dating men not knowing who Kara was left me further lost in a downward spiral.

    I spent my last dime traveling by greyhound to see different men, from state to state dating men that could care less about me. I was searching for love in all of the wrong places. I allowed men that I dated and talked to, to treat me any way they wanted. I was disrespected, cheated on, and experienced verbal and emotional abuse. Up until age 23 I did not value, nor did I know my self-worth. Thus forth, I allowed men to use my body for their sexual pleasure and I allowed myself to be manipulated into thinking these men actually cared about me.

During 18-23 I came across many "past times" that I would talk to online. A past time means someone to talk to or text, just to "past the time." Usually past times were rebounds or just sexting buddies or men I used for the time being. I tried to hurt some of the past times the way my exes hurt me, but it never worked. I did not care about myself, nor did I respect myself or love myself enough to realize the downward and dangerous spiral I was on. I allowed men to degrade my body in almost every way possible, during 18-23 I was becoming numb to the pain, I simply did not care.

All the while I was miserable and hurting. I looked to men to feel beautiful about all of my insecurities, in which I hated. When one of my exes said my stretchmarks did not bother him, it made me feel pretty. As opposed to a guy I once talked to that thought they were ugly and disgusting. I thrived off the comments from other men, to any little comment that would easily boost or lower my self-esteem. I allowed the words of men to stay engrained in my mind, whether they were helping or hurting me, I allowed them in. I placed my identity and self-worth in the hands of other men.

I had no idea of what a good man was or looked like, this was something I thought a father was supposed to teach his daughter. My older half-brother was the only male that I knew cared about me and my sister, and as I got older our relationship grew. He was at every birthday, graduation, celebration, and he has such a big heart. This was the only positive male figure I had growing up. I only went off of brief conversations with my mom and what I saw in the movies about good guys. I love my mother for everything she taught me about womanhood and life, but there were things about men I wish I knew from having a consistent positive father or male figure in my life.

I also acted out and sometimes treated men badly with my words to hurt them, as the saying goes hurt people hurt people. I was naive and young when I started dating my first boyfriend at 17 years old, I was saying I love you to someone without even knowing what the definition of love was. I never been in love, I was only in love with trying to fulfill a void of not having a father to love me. I did not respect, nor love myself to understand my beauty and worth. I remember crying over every ex, thinking my world was over, and even planning to commit suicide over a man leaving my life. I was so lost and every tear I cried over those men, were the same tears I cried at night wishing I had a father.

I know there is no such thing as a perfect family or perfect parent, but I never stopped longing for the love of my father. I will never forget the times we spoke and I would easily hear his tone of voice change. There was also a time when I had a phone conversation with my dad and he said I looked like Chaka Khan, because of the afro I had in the pictures me and my sister mailed him and he said that I looked beautiful. When I heard that I did not know how to feel, because many times we talked he sounded so angry and bitter, as he talked about things that had nothing to do with a father building a healthy relationship with his daughter.

As I stated previously, I looked to other men in order to feel beautiful and I looked to men to feel good about myself. For so many years I struggled, not addressing the issues that I had, from the void within my heart, the void of not having a father. I use to dream of having a father that would tell me how amazing and beautiful I was. I wanted a father to push me on the swings, and play outside with me, like my mother played with me and my sister at the park all the time when we were little. To taking us to the circus and everything else. I dreamed about having a father tell me how proud of me he was and how much he loved me. All the times teachers doubted me and people said I was retarded or slow, yet I finished college with honors and began writing this book at 21 years old.

All the nights I stayed up late typing papers and ran on coffee fumes, to where I did not think I was going to even finish college, because money was scarce, but with financial aid, I was able to finish school. When I debated for hours whether I was going to use my last bit of money to catch a cab down to Huntington beach lake in Cleveland and lay down in the water and go to sleep, I often thought of this plan after I graduated college.

To the time when I wanted to take my full bottle of ibuprofen 600mg with the cheap bottle of vodka my older male friend brought me from CVS, I had hidden under my dorm room bed to go to sleep. Those nights I wanted to go to sleep for good and never wake up, I just wanted the pain to go away. So many nights contemplating suicide and weeping until my eyes were puffy blood shot red and the middle of my throat felt permanently swollen. I choked on tears longing for my fathers hug, wondering if he would even show up to my funeral if I did kill myself.

I wanted my father to protect me from the strange man that offered me a ride at the bus stop when I was 11 years old headed to school. I wanted my father to be one of those dads with the baseball bat that would do anything to shield his daughter from harm. I wanted my father to protect me from the man that followed me into my job, as I was walking to work when I was 15 years old. I wanted my father to wipe the tears from my eyes, from every ex that broke my heart, to every person that ever called me ugly and made me feel like crap. I wanted a father to hold me after every man used my body and left me.

As a little girl going to church I use to pray for my father all the time, from prayer lines to Sunday school. The deacon or minster would ask, "Do you have any prayer request?" my response "I just wanna pray for my father." I was only 9 years old, and I use to think prayer request are for when you really want something or really want to receive something. I thought the more I put in prayer requests for him, then maybe God would send him to America. At that age I had my mom, sister, and toys, but I always wanted my father. Then I use to pray for him, because I wanted God to take away all the anger I heard in his voice every time we spoke.

I hated my father for his broken promises and not picking up the phone to call me during some of the best and worst moments in my life. I hated the selfishness and cockiness I always heard in his voice. I hated my father for the way he spoke about my mother and the way he spoke to me, my sister, and half-brother. I wanted to be somebodies princess, therefore I settled for hearing these words from men to fulfill that void, every man I ever dated were temporary void fillers, when the one man I wanted to hear those words from and mean it was my father. I longed to hear all of the things a great father instills in his child. I never wanted money or any materialistic items from my father, whether he could provide for me or not.

All I wanted was for my father to speak life into me and mean it, I wanted to know my fathers favorite color, favorite movie, and what his life was like growing up in Liberia. I wanted to know what his passion and goals were when he was younger. Where did he go to school, and all the many questions I had about life in Liberia and America before his departure to Canada. Yet, I knew nothing about this man that was my biological father. I only knew what my mother told me and the things I searched on the internet about Liberia, and information that came up whenever I googled his name.

All the questions I ask my mom about dating, her favorite food recipes, and her experiences growing up in the Hough area. In the impoverished inner city of Cleveland, Ohio and not having proper winter coats to go to school, and how hard times got as the oldest of 7 other siblings, she has told me plenty of her childhood stories. However, I thirsted to know my fathers story, I had so many questions for my father, I wanted to connect with him. I wondered if we liked the same foods, same books, was he a coffee addict like I was, and basically what we had in common.

Through dating, these were all of the questions I asked other men, not realizing these same questions are questions I wanted to ask my father. It was not until I began seeking out God whole heartedly that I was able to forgive, heal, and understand my true beauty. God is slowly filling the void of an absent father within my heart and I can feel it. I wanted one of those fairy tale fathers from the movies and I did not realize I was becoming angry and bitter like my father. Growing up he always talked about family members as if it were a constant competition, which always made me sick to my stomach.

It made me sick to my stomach, because my mother never raised me or my sister to be competitive, jealous, or envious of one another. My mother raised me and my sister to always support and love one another, especially family. Every time

I spoke to my father, he always expressed his issues and bitterness towards some of his own siblings, that had nothing to do with me. Then in 2015 was the last straw and I simply gave up on all communication. When I called him and basically said I am trying to get to know you and build a relationship with you, his response was you're an adult now, aren't you still living with your mother, and a very nasty attitude of why are you calling me, before he began ranting about stuff that had nothing to do with me.

It was at that moment that I realized my father has failed to address his mental health, in which he refuses to ever get the proper help he needs to move forward. My father never once apologized for not being in me or my sisters life. My father was absent mentally, financially, physically, emotionally, and all of the above. He was and still is a stranger to me. Then two days after my birthday September 16th of this year 2016, I woke up to texts from him calling me stupid and useless, because when he texted me prior, I told him that he needs to address his mental health issues and to no longer contact me.

I kept the entire text thread saved in my phone, because I've done nothing wrong, and no father, let alone an absent one at that, should ever text or talk to their child that way. The only way he got my new number was through my half-brother. His toxic words are very dangerous, that I want no part of him in my life. All I do is pray for him and love him from a distance. The only father I ever knew always sounded angry and bitter, as if he refuses to forgive anyone whose ever done him wrong.

He has a temper, that I will never forget hearing over the phone, through his yelling about things that have nothing to do with me. Then one day when I was about 20 years old, my sister said you are acting like our dad, when I would get mad, it was then that I realized I was harboring the same anger and unforgiveness towards people that once hurt me. Underneath all of that I know there is a heart there and hopefully one day God will heal my fathers heart completely. Through counseling, writing, and praying I was able to continue healing from any resentment I had towards my father and other people. Until I finally released it all to God, it is all a process.

All of the nice words in the beginning of a relationship are the same words I wanted to hear my father say. Whether you have an absent parent or absent family members, you must value yourself as a great individual. The more you say it, practice it, and believe it the more it will come to life. I included this piece about my absent father, because his absence was apart of my journey towards healing, forgiveness, letting go, and discovering my True Beauty and worth.

If your story is similar to mine, all you can do is release it to God and move forward. At some point you have to wake up and refuse to be a victim, and fight. The day I began defining my own definition of True Beauty, was the day I stopped being a victim to other peoples words. No matter the circumstances in which you grew up, you are beautiful and worthy. I often hear women discussing how badly they want or need a man, as well as seeking validation from men, "He said I look way better than her or he said I'm the best he's ever had." All of this to boost confidence or an already large ego. Whatever the case may be, you must not lose who you are and what you stand for, all for the approval of men.

It is important to know your true beauty and validate this for yourself, as opposed to ending up like one of the women we see fighting with multiple women over one man. I am guilty of this too because one of my exes that I thought God said was the one (I was wrong once again), I sent mean messages to him and his current girlfriend, because I was so upset that he moved on three weeks after we broke up and flaunted it on social media. I felt inferior, I knew she was prettier than me, because my insecurities said she was pettier than me. Do not be the female that I was, angry, bitter, and heartbroken.

You must forgive, heal, give it to God and apologize to those parties involved if you ever hurt another female, male, or ex out of being hurt. I apologized back then for my mean words, because

I always felt horrible shortly after and the guilt would stay with me, until I apologized. However, as women, we must kill these type of thoughts immediately. Also, you do not need to be the female dating multiple men just to feel a sense of empowerment or feel the need to crush the double standard, of "since he can do it then so can I."

Yes, you can do anything you put your mind to, but attempt actions that move you towards your personal growth and freedom, not just to compete with a man. Love yourself enough to walk away, stay single for a while, unplug from social media, change your phone number if you have to, treat yourself, and have fun loving who you are. I worked out, wrote in my diary and journals, changed my numbers, deleted email addresses, blocked people, all because I chose to love me and never return to people that did not love me or value me the way I did.

For those that are not single, do you know who you are without him and what is your identity outside of a man, or is your entire existence resting in his hands. It was not until I reached 24 that I realized from age 18-23 I kept allowing men and boys to use my physical body as their play toy. I was just a physical object that was good enough for their pleasure, and I thought back to all the years I was so wrapped up in their opinions and standards of beauty, that it became the norm. A false norm that is also perpetuated through our media, as we see men and boys choosing the prettiest or best looking as opposed to looking for inner qualities, which is not true for all, but is for some males.

Through studies and opinion, some say that men are physical creatures by nature, as it seems gender roles and double standards exist in this world. It is an awesome world when progression takes place, yet our society is failing to produce real and true definitions of good men and good people. I see why the "bad boy" image is constantly glorified as opposed to the good guy image and the image of girls and women gravitating towards the bad boy image. Everyone obtains their own preference, yet it is not okay for certain negative or bad behaviors to be praised as good. I also noticed how some men of all statuses in society make disgusting and derogatory comments about girls and women on social media.

I am not blaming males in this chapter because some women do the same. Every day we let men determine the worth and value of the female body. For example, in an all-male dominated hip hop industry, artists daily express their preferences of skin color and body type. These male artists also choose women that fit their standards of what they now call "bad b*****s." There are so many male artists within the hip hop industry that showcase the continued boxed definition of beauty. From males that prefer yellow bones, exotic women to foreign women, basically another term for exotic.

Meaning the more exotic or foreign she appears to be, that equates to her superior beauty. Sometimes if I am reading a blog post or headline, I cannot help but to laugh at the subtitles of which new celebrity male is dating an "exotical female or how he upgraded to an exotic foreign beauty." Then when I see the pictures of these women, I only see physical equal beauty in which we all possess, none greater or lesser. In almost every rap song I heard growing up I always heard the words yellow bone.

To this day there is this obsession with light skin and European features as being the standard for beauty. Some people may see no issue with always portraying the main or lead girls as light, white, thin, or perfect coke bottled shape, but as society is evolving more people are understanding how important representation is. Especially for girls and women, to be able to see themselves in all professions and walks of life in a positive light. No matter how many surgeries you get to look "exotic" you will still have days where you feel ugly and there is no such thing as exotic beauty according to my definition of true beauty.

As people we can't let other peoples opinions become the sole definers of our identity, along with letting one mans words define our beauty. The opinions of masses of men have power to define a false definition of beauty concerning women. This is why I do not download certain music or use words that insult me or other people as well as other women. We often let men dictate the logical decisions in which we as women are just as capable of making ourselves. I often hear men and boys talking about women as they would a pair of tennis shoes. Once you wear them a few times, throw them away, then one buys another pair of shoes to shine up and show off.

You are not his pair of shoes to be walked on, used, worn, and thrown away. From hearing men brag about their sexual partners, to who's ugly and who's the prettiest female. I have overheard vulgar to very descriptive conversations, that men have had in public about women and girls they are interested in or not. I am not saying all men are "bad boys" or try to define a womans beauty. However, there are a lot of men in our world that behave this way directly and indirectly, as opposed to some men that do not realize their destructive behavior towards women. Men are able to get away with what we as women allow them to get away with.

We have the power to say no and act consistently on those healthy choices, we have the power to say "I will not allow you to abuse me with your words, nor your physical actions, I will fight back and leave, you do not own me." In our society there is constant pressure for women to look completely flawless in order to be considered beautiful by some men and women. However, in order to be sexy or even considered beautiful a female has to show a form of cleavage. These sort of men that verbally, physically, or sexually abuse and exploit girls and women against their will are not men.

I chose this as one of the definers of beauty, because I have seen the countless news stories of girls and boys committing suicide based upon past and present male bullies, boyfriends, or ex boyfriends that told them to kill themselves or leaked private pictures of their partner online. I can relate to that last one, because after me and one of my exes broke up, we later got into an argument and he threatened to leak private photos of me that I sent him. I made time for men that did not make time for me and I chased men that wouldn't dare pursue me.

I know the feeling of a mental and emotional breakdown, when the man you love disappears or breaks up with you and you feel like you are suffocating. I have been there and with God, he will bring you out of that storm. I allowed so many men to define me that I used to hate looking at mirrors, because if I did I would stare at myself too long and feel so uncomfortable finding new flaws on my body. I know how it feels to feel worthless and powerless to a male that is repeatedly putting you down with his words.

Words are dangerous and powerful, but again they are only powerful when we give them power. If you are in this situation now, get out or seek help, any way you can, you must fight! As girls and women take the power out of derogatory and abusive words, know who you are and do not respond to anything that you know you are not. I noticed how some boys and men are quick to call a female a slut, whore, b*tch, or ho, all while doing the same promiscuous behaviors of sleeping around. It does not matter what you wear, who you are or what you do, some men and women use words like slut, whore, or b*tch to tear you down. I have been called all of those names, once by a male I worked with and overheard him call me a hoe, this was when I was working as a package handler.

I also dealt with an ex who called me a hoe and b*tch when we were breaking up. To another past time male that called me a b*tch via text and on the phone when I did not do what he wanted. I am tired of hearing some men degrade women on a daily basis, as if it is a new norm, along with women and girls who openly embrace being degraded.

If you can degrade, exploit, and disrespect the female body which bore you, then one does not deserve to call himself a man. If you are a female like myself that grew up without a father, do not accept any of the negative statistics that researchers state you will fall victim to.

Discover and embrace your worth now, do not wait for a man to come along and be your prince charming to tell you all the wonderful and miraculous things about you. You have to finally be brave enough to look into the mirror and speak life over yourself. Any void you are missing from an absence in your life, seek God to fulfill that void. When I prayed, fasted, and cried out to God night after night, my pillow was soaked and I screamed for peace in my heart.

It was then that I was able to forgive my father and any male who left invisible deep wounds that only God could heal. Forgiveness is the only way that you will be able to move forward and live out your true beauty. From the last three M's media, materials, and men I have one last plea. My last plea to girls and women is to NEVER let any man or boy define your beauty. Not only your beauty but your worth as an individual and powerful female in this world. No matter what obstacles life may throw your way, always remember your body, heart, and mind are priceless.

As my mother always taught me, we as women are not for sale, because we are truly precious and priceless. I have always stuck with this quote in my head as I construct my own definition of true beauty for all women and girls to understand and grasp as a positive definition in which you can apply to your daily life.

Chapter 6

Beauty Hurts: Comparing and Competing

In our world beauty is a superficial definition that is placed upon a pedestal and it comes with a cost. Due to science and technology surgeons can almost do any procedure to enhance, restructure, or create a so called perfect image.

If one was a victim of a tragedy or accident, and needed reconstructive surgery, I completely understand. In contrast to being made into a human doll by getting reconstructive surgery to look like a Barbie doll or to look like a particular celebrity, this is something I am completely opposed to. I often hear and see this notion of beauty equating to pain, and if you want to look good then you have to suffer. You have to suffer in 8 inch heels and not be able to breath in a corset and body shapers that slowly cut off your oxygen. I understand how high heels can be very uncomfortable after long hours of standing, walking, or dancing.

I remember the first time I wore heels to my 9th grade homecoming, although they were not that high my feet were on fire, all I was use to wearing were flats, tennis shoes, and sandals. I also remember the first time I wore false eyelashes to my high school prom and they were so uncomfortable that I wanted to rip them off as soon as I started feeling the discomfort. Many women like myself have experienced the physical pain of "looking beautiful." The question once again is who are you trying to look beautiful for and do you really feel beautiful.

There is a major difference between looking and feeling beautiful. Beauty does not have to hurt, I realized that it hurts when you allow it to hurt. Even when people around you talk about the way you look, or dress, you have to remember that you are beautiful. Do not allow anyone or anything to darken the beautiful light that you possess from within. I often hear women and girls constantly comparing and competing to who is beautiful and who is not. It is so common in our society, that comparing and competing is becoming toxic.

Comparing and competing further leads to beauty hurting, especially when you compare yourself to other beautiful girls and women in the room, or the ones you see on your social media timeline. I have often noticed and overheard other women that will compliment another on her beauty and looks, but follow it with a negative comment of "she's not that cute or she think she is all that." When you compare you are setting your self-esteem up for failure and you are placing their beauty on a pedestal. Once you do that you are placing their physical appearance on a higher level, therefore automatically making your physical appearance inferior and not good enough.

For example, when you say "her nose and hair are like mine, therefore I am just as pretty as she is, or if I get blonde extensions and lip injections then I will look prettier. I believe that comparing ultimately leads to self-destruction and the further destruction of one's self esteem. As well as competing, because competing is very parallel to comparing. The major difference is you now are competing to be the prettiest girl in the room, or the girl with biggest this or that, or the girl with the most money. As well as competing with those that you constantly compare yourself to. Competing and comparing destroys self-worth, as you constantly place your worth in the hands of other people by comparing and competing.

You are giving them that power over your true beauty, which is from within. I, like many women have made this mistake of comparing and competing when it came to beauty and physical appearance. It is okay to admire, like, or compliment another based upon their physical appearance, but do not compare and compete with that person or those people that you admire. I understand that people often say impersonation or imitation is a form of flattery, but it can also become a form of idolizing.

So think to yourself, who have you been idolizing or admiring, and why? I believe in having role models, heroes, and looking up to people that have inspired you. However, the real question is, do you inspire you, do you admire you, and who exactly are you? These are the questions you need to ask yourself, in making sure that you know you are truly worthy and beautiful. This means you are simply beautiful by being yourself and knowing your worth resides in your hands. I think to myself why does beauty hurt and why does pain have to be attached to physical beauty.

Heels may hurt, and eyelashes may be annoying, but as human beings and women we have control over what we wear and what we allow into our minds. However, when you compare and compete over physical appearance, you are only adding to the internal hurt. The internal hurt you are causing yourself and hurt you may be bringing upon someone else. Once you compare your flaws to someone elses you are further displaying your insecurities and lack of self-esteem. By comparing yourself to other people you will gain nothing. For example, "my nose is smaller and my hair is longer than hers so I look better than her." Even if you do not compare yourself to those girls or women, you may still find yourself competing to be better than her.

If you do not see it and get ahold of finding your true beauty, then comparing and competing may be a continuous cycle for you. Beauty should not hurt, but comparing and competing further adds to that hurt. As I have stated before that as girls and women, we can be extremely mean to one another and just plain flat out mean girls. Especially when it comes to judging another female based upon her looks, which made me think of this notion of "beauty bullies." As women we can be so critical and judgmental towards each other, and I understand what that is like.

Some of the harshest things I have heard concerning my appearance and abilities have come from the mouths of fellow women. Sometimes comments happen so fast, you don't process it until after it happens. Like the time I was at a festival and I remember walking past a girl, and as I past, I heard her say "what is wrong with her face."

Constantly being called ugly and funny looking from complete strangers, and girls that I encountered on campus, in class, and women that I worked with. Do not be one of those girls tearing down one another just because you can.

It sometimes seems as if the bullying is getting worse, as we constantly see women criticizing one another, while being praised for this behavior. Are you being a beauty bully, tearing down other women from head to toe or beauty police by harshly judging, as well as constantly comparing and competing? Do not allow the media or anyone to fool you into believing that you are ugly, or that you must have body enhancements to be beautiful.

As a Christian do not allow the enemy, the devil to play tricks on your mind. In our world we have competitions everywhere, according to some people, life is all about competition. I agree that in life we are forced to compete, from jobs, competing to have the highest GPA to having the top selling business in your city or the world. Whatever you are working towards or competing with, I challenge you to re-evaluate and ask yourself is this worth competing over. As I remember my mother once saying to pick and choose my battles in life. Beauty does not have to be a constant competition, nor does being beautiful have to be a competition. Being beautiful does not and should not be a battle, true beauty is effortless, it is not envious, jealous, nor competitive.

It is effortless beauty when I wake up, shower, pull my hair back, get dressed and go. Minus the makeup, and hours of doing too much just to go to the store. Like I said, there is nothing wrong with looking fly, but True beauty is effortless. Be confidently beautiful and walk in boldness as you embrace your true beauty. As women we must rise above the worlds definition of beauty and being so self-absorbed, be more than physically beautiful, be more than just another pretty face.

Take a look in the mirror and erase all of your flaws aloud. Look in the mirror and tell yourself I am not ugly, I embrace my stretchmarks, I embrace my acne, I embrace my weight, and I am beautiful! Compare and compete to be a better you. Do not compare your flaws, erase the flaws from your brain and embrace them as beauty blessings. Compete with only yourself to overcome your challenges, when I say compete I mean to truly challenge yourself to overcome obstacles in your life. The same obstacles that are prohibiting you from becoming a confident person and walking in your true beauty.

In order to walk in your true beauty, you have to erase in order to embrace; therefore erase all negativity, all of the 3 M's, and any barrier that is holding you back from embracing your true beauty. I could no longer ignore the issues involved with comparing and competition, because I see it happen daily. When it comes to beauty, are you a compare and compete kind of person or have you ever compared or competed when it came to beauty. When I looked back to my teen and early college days, I was more of a comparer. Then as I really thought back to my childhood I always compared my physical features to celebrities, popular girls, and pageant models to try and feel beautiful. The only thing I use to like about my physical appearance was my long hair, but I use to hate the thick tight coiled hair, that the world viewed as not as beautiful (Not True).

When I was younger I grew sensitized to seeing models with long hair, so I thought long straight hair was the standard to follow. I thank God that as I got older I learned to redefine my own definition of beauty. If you are comparing and competing, then end the senseless battle. No one is perfect and there is no such thing as a scale or standard of beauty. As I re-evaluate my definition of true beauty, it is crucially important that you eliminate certain ideas, words, and phrases from your brain.

I often hear and see words such as prettiest, basic, classic, ugliest, exotic, and words that I have mentioned previously. The words some use to build up or tear down our fellow sisters, whether it be in person or online. I will never forget the comments about my head, face, hair, and physical appearance from childhood throughout my adulthood. To a random man who joked about my feet with his coworker, when I was at the greyhound terminal, returning from visiting an ex. To being at a weekend camp pretending to be sleep, while a bunk bed room full of female classmates joke and laugh about you being so slow and weird.

That was 6th grade when I attended a weekend school camp trip, I just remember wanting to go home after that night, I cried silently in my bunk. I know what that is like and the pain of put downs are immeasurable. If you have been bullied or taunted because of your physical appearance I stand with you and I encourage you to keep holding on and know that you are beautiful. God did not make any mistakes when he made you. All beauty is equal beauty, every female possesses different and unique qualities that make them beautiful. Comparing and competing further leaves you in bondage.

When you finally open your heart and mind to changing your lenses and finally view beauty as internal and outer beauty as equal, you will no longer feel the need to compare and compete. Stop comparing and competing with your fellow sisters, friends, family members, co-workers, complete strangers, celebrities, and those that you admire. Be beautiful being yourself and be the most beautiful girl and most beautiful woman that you know you are and can be. I say most which means being the best you that only you can be. You cannot do that when you are constantly comparing and competing with other people.

When I finally looked in the mirror, after praying, fasting, working out, and taking a break from social media, I was able to continue writing and working on becoming a better me. The journey to discovering your true beauty begins with you and fully loving who you are as a beautiful human being. In 2012 of September when I began writing this book, I was 20 years old about to turn 21 in September. My journey to finding my true beauty started in my adulthood during my junior year of college. I say this because it is never too late to start your journey to finding your true beauty.

Even girls and women who may fall into this boxed definition of beauty, some of them are struggling with low self-esteem and may have never felt beautiful. No matter what color or shape you are, so many women struggle with body image and low self-esteem. What I saw as ugly on myself, someone else could be admiring, we all struggle with things we may dislike about our physical appearance. I am writing these words so that all girls and women can discover their True Beauty. Thankfully, the times are changing. I love the fact that companies and many individuals are challenging the global standard of beauty.

The "boxed beauty" definition I mentioned earlier of not all beauty being thin, long hair, fair, white skin, light skin, or small features is the standard. From bloggers, girls, to models of color, many girls and women are speaking out and defining what real beauty is. They are doing this in their own way. As I continue to see commercials and reading about the Dove study that showed only 4% of women consider themselves to be beautiful. This statistic further displayed that we a have a global problem of girls and women struggling with low self-esteem, lack of confidence, and not just with their physical appearance.

Knowing and finding your true beauty is so much more than joining a movement of women and girls recreating their own definition of beauty. A definition of beauty that says you are beautiful being you and true beauty without limitations. Society says your freckles, wide nose, acne, big lips, gap teeth, large hips, albino skin, physical disability, tightly coiled hair, round stomach, big ears, dark skin, and short hair, are all limitations that do not equate to beauty. But today is the day that you tell society to shove it! Tell them that you are beautifully flawed and that you are flawed beyond perfection, why?

Because there is no such thing as perfection, except for perfectly re touched photos (lol). God loves you and God did not make any mistakes when he made you. I will never get tired of saying this.

Chapter 7

What is your Beauty Worth?

So, as I discussed earlier about my mother teaching me to value myself as precious and priceless. It is very important that you all as girls and women view yourself the same way and as valuable human beings.

However, you cannot view yourself as precious and priceless, if you do not know your worth. Just as one would think about the value, cost, and worth of certain items. It is really important that you ask yourself, what are you worth? Is your dignity, self- respect, integrity, character, and morals priceless or do they come with a specific cost? True beauty is feeling worthy and knowing your worth. I did not always know, nor did I value my worth. As I said before that I always felt ugly, worthless, and talentless. Reflect and ask yourself do you feel worthy and how much is your beauty worth.

Is your beauty for sale, along with your body? When I was around 19 years old and I was just out of my first relationship, my self-esteem was at an all-time low. I was serial dating and bouncing from relationship to relationship and talking to men online from around the world, which I had no business talking to. After my first failed relationship, and the already preexisting low self-esteem issues I felt even more worthless, and I sold my beauty for love, attention, and affection. During this downward spiral I was not only giving my body away but my heart, time, and all of myself to people that did not care about me.

When you are empty and worn out, the worthless feelings further kick in. I was tired of being belittled, walked on, and made fun of for the way I looked. Which is another reason I am in the process of taking a long break from dating, in order to redefine and improve myself. Knowing your worth starts with loving who you are and loving the individual God made you to be. That is what True Beauty is all about, my definition of beauty is valuing your worth. Once you value your worth, you respect, protect, and cherish that worth, which is who you are.

Whether it be working out, praying, fasting, meditating, studying, taking classes, or anything you have to do to become a more beautiful you. You can be beautiful and just as worthy as your fellow sisters. No matter what our world says is worthy and respectable, you have to discover and define your worth. Take time to define your worth and what your beauty is worth. Do not allow anyone else to define your worth. It is really important that you ask yourself, do you feel valuable and do you feel worthy. When I allowed men to use my body, I exploited and opened myself up to men that did not care about me nor my worth.

That is why I continued to act out how I felt, which was worthless, I didn't know my worth nor did I value it, therefore I still allowed people to abuse my worth. Back then I based my worth upon the 3 M's and I allowed everything and everyone else to define my worth and true beauty. It is very important to look at what you are basing your worth upon, and are you selling or prostituting your worth. This is why I reiterate the importance of loving yourself and loving your worth. Think back to the time that you felt worthless and then think back to all of the times in which you felt worthy.

Where were you, how old were you, what were you thinking, and feeling? Who or what in your life made you feel important, special, loved, or worthy.

When I was younger my mom and sister always made me feel loved and worthy. My mom and sister always taught me to be myself and they were the ones that told me I was beautiful when I never felt like it. All the while I hid behind fake smiles and thick makeup. Even if you do not have anyone in your life that uplifts you or makes you feel worthy, always remember you are worthy, you are important, and you are priceless, because God says you are.

The true beauty that you possess is like no other, it is unique and it is you. I challenge you to own your worthiness and walk in the true beauty that is from within. No matter what anyone has said to doubt you or take away from you. You must remember that you are still alive and still strong, therefore embrace and cherish who you are. Our past does not define our worth, God defines your worth and purpose in this world. By knowing your worth, you will begin to grow in the inner areas of your life, meaning spiritually and mentally. When I began to define my worth and know my true beauty, I was growing spiritually, emotionally, and mentally.

No matter if people called me ugly or said negative comments about me, I knew my worth. I knew that I did not have to answer nor respond to things that did not define me. It is a journey that you have to be willing to take at some point in your life and no matter what age you are, it is not too late. By knowing your worth, you have to look at yourself deeply, identify all of the qualities inner and outer that make you beautiful and worthy. Once you discover and find your worth, you will be able to walk in that worth. Every time I hear or see something negative about myself I block it out and it will be a struggle but you can do it.

One day you will have the courage to say I know my worth and I know the beauty within my worth. Your true beauty is worthy and a beauty that is different from society's definition of beauty that is obsessed with one's physical appearance. Are you teaching your friends, sisters, mothers, daughters, aunts, grandmothers, that they are worthy and telling them that they are beautiful? Identify what makes you beautiful and find strength within your beauty. At 21 years old when I realized I was determined to be a writer, I took pride in my gift and talent.

I did not realize that I was writing stories and poems since I was 9 years old and God blessed with the gift to write. God gave me my voice through my pen and pencil. As I type these words, I no longer feel like that quiet, shy girl that was once bullied. Writing gave me confidence and made me feel beautiful, because it was something I was good at. Poems, songs, short stories, visions, all these things coming from my large imagination. Realizing I wanted to be an advocate for anti-bullying and building self-esteem amongst girls and women that struggled in those same areas as I did and simply having a heart to help people made me feel beautiful. There are many things that make you beautiful and you must start making a list of those things.

Every time I looked in the mirror, I questioned my beauty and worth. From bathroom mirrors to dressing room mirrors, I was questioning everything about my physical appearance. I hated what I saw in the mirror, yet I pretended to be beautiful online and acted as if I had confidence. Do not be afraid to look in the mirror or step on the scale. You can change your physical appearance as well as change the number on a scale. However, the most important thing you must change is your mindset and embrace who you are right now. Embrace being pretty when you look in the mirror and as soon as you walk out the door.

My older sister is in the process of losing weight, because she does not like her current size. I remind her that no matter what size she is, that she too is beautiful. This is because she possesses true inner beauty. Once you determine who you are, it is important that you own it and exemplify being that great beautiful girl or woman. As humans we have the tendency to always point out his or her flaws first. This is why I challenge you to find the pretty within your flaws and redefine them as beautiful.

When you say I think I'm beautiful, the "think" comes from doubt. You have to believe and know that you are beautiful. Do not allow negative thoughts or negative people stop you from feeling confident about who you are. As well as uplifting your loved ones and female friends in letting them know that they are beautiful and worthy. My definition of beauty, true beauty is to spread a light of encouragement to all women and girls struggling to love themselves. My mother, sister, and grandmother were the first women to tell me I was beautiful and remind me of my self-worth. I was blessed and fortune to have them in my life growing up.

For those women and girls that grew up without a mother, grandmother, sister, aunt, great grandmother, God says you are beautiful. From one woman to another, you are beautiful and worthy. For women and girls that grew up with these women in your life and never heard those words,

God says you are beautiful and I say you are beautiful. For those women that have been battered, incarcerated, homeless, disabled, scorned, abused, lied to, mistreated, or ever faced any obstacle or trial in your life, always remember God says you are beautiful. God loves us unconditionally and he is not judging us on our past failures and sins. Forgive yourself, try your best to love and value yourself the same way God loves and values you, unconditionally.

Chapter 8

Reborn Beauty

What does God say about beauty? When I read my bible, I know that God is after our hearts and could care less about our physical appearance. After googling this question many scriptures came up, *"Your beauty should not come from outward adornment, such as braided hair and the wearing of gold jewelry and fine clothes. Instead, it should be that of your inner self, the unfading beauty of a gentle and quiet spirit, which is of great worth in God's sight. For this is the way the holy women of the past who put their hope in God used to make themselves beautiful." 1 Peter 3:3–5*. One of the scriptures that my mother read to me growing up was *Psalms 139:14 "I praise you because I am fearfully and wonderfully made, your works are wonderful. I know that full well."*

There are many great scriptures on Gods definition of beauty, but one last scripture to remember is *"You are altogether beautiful, my darling; there is no flaw in you" Song of Solomon 4:7.*

I came to the common-sense definition that beauty is truly something from within and it is up to you discover what those things are. The everlasting beauty from within your heart and mind is what matters most. Those are the two places in which a womans true beauty can be discovered. A womans sense of empowerment should not only come from only taking off her clothes and bending over for a top magazine cover.

That empowerment should come from her mind and how she uses it to truly transform the world for the better, without losing her dignity and sophistication. Beauty from within should never be swept under the rug, because it is what sets us apart as women. I have met plenty of beautiful women and girls, their outside physical appearance was attractive. However, on the inside some of these same girls and women were some of the meanest bullies and extremely cruel individuals I had ever encountered. There are beautiful girls all around the world, but our inside is what makes us distinctively unique. Beauty is so much more than models, celebrities, fair skin, long hair extensions, coke bottled body frames, and it is so much more than looking perfect, which is a myth.

We must not allow media to trick our minds with this false definition of perfection, a concept that does not exist, as we all have made mistakes in life. As women our physical attributes do not solely define our beauty. Pageant queens, models, and celebrities do not represent the standard of TRUE beauty, because we as women and girls are all equally beautiful. No matter the race, religion, class, or background, always know that you are a beautiful girl and you are a beautiful queen.

Whether you grew up in poverty, a tomboy, wearing a hijab, scars, frizzy to curly hair, thick glasses, dark or brown skin, full figured, blue or dark brown eyes or not, you too are beautiful. You are beautiful because of your inside first and always remember that is all that matters.

The world judges you based on your physical appearance, but as long as you know your true beauty that is all that matters. Every female obtains their own story and our physical appearance is not a symbol of our TRUE beauty. Our physical appearance is only one attribute, the mind and heart are symbols of our TRUE beauty. I hope that you all understand my definition of beauty, which is true beauty that only shines from within you.

The 3 M's do not define our beauty so we must not let them continue to over power or weigh us down with their negative and false definitions of OUR beauty. My definition of beauty is based upon characteristics of the heart and mind. True beauty is self-less, honest, humble, respectful, sophisticated, wise, intelligent, hardworking, and so much more. True beauty embodies the characteristics that all women and girls should strive to one day obtain. As well as being hardworking, independent, strong minded, and compassionate women are just as great. Be bad in killing with kindness and allowing your success to speak for itself. One can be a strong, powerful, and a dominant woman without degrading herself.

In a world that is raping, abusing, and demeaning our bodies, we as women and girls have the right to stand up and say no we will not allow ourselves to be dominated. Your true beauty and physical attributes are not worth any amount of money in the world, because you are priceless. Whether you are a teenage mother, teacher, stay at home mother, soldier, beautician, waitress, CEO, physician, a survivor, engineer, photographer, athlete, author, or whatever your title may be, just remember you too are beautiful. Your school or job title does not define your identity as a truly beautiful female in this world.

As humans we often let our job, status, or position titles define who we are. This is not true because as I have stated, we as women are more than our titles and physical attributes. These physical attributes are clothes, hair, shoes, eyes, and other outer aspects that mean nothing because in God's eyes he created us equally beautiful. After you read this, think of five non-physical characteristics or attributes that make you beautiful! Now write them down and post them on your mirror or somewhere that you will view this list on a daily basis. Beauty is not fighting, malicious, and tearing down your fellow female sisters. Beauty is not mean mugging your fellow sisters just because.

True Beauty is complementing her instead of competing with her or comparing your beauty to hers. True Beauty is working together as women and girls to EMPOWER one another, while not letting men strip us of that great power. How can we fight against those that try to take away our rights, silence our voices, while they exploit our bodies as we continue to divide ourselves? No we won't all get along, but we can do our very best to respect and accept our differences. There is nothing wrong with making new female friends and sisters that you click and bond with over music, religion, fashion, or anything.

I challenge you to make new healthy lifelong friendships and a sisterhood in which you encourage one another to live and walk in their true beauty. I only hope to bridge the gaps between races, sizes, classes, and religions of women around the world. One uniting factor is that we as women are all equally beautiful, and there is no one female whom is greater. I want to raise the esteem of all of those women and girls in which society deem as unattractive and ugly girls. Whether she is fighting breast cancer or fighting off bullies in her classroom she too is beautiful. The gray hair wheelchair bound, wrinkles, is just as beautiful as a freshman attending her first day of high school. As I said previously, to the dark skinned, albino, or to the woman with burn scars, they are all equally beautiful.

Throughout my life experiences I realized that so many women of all colors, Black, White, Hispanic, Asian/Pacific Islander, Biracial, and all shades of women are struggling to feel beautiful. As I state throughout this book, you have to discover your True Beauty and own it! Do not be a victim of the boxed definition of beauty. Fight back and declare that you are not ugly, nor worthless. Positive daily affirmations is a start, but you have to define a healthy positive body image and mindset for yourself. There is no need to have a war between aged beauty versus young beauty, as we see competitions of women dying to look and stay young, as well as women feeling ashamed to state their age.

I believe many great things come with age, if one allows and embraces growth into their life. Wisdom, boldness, strength, and many more positive qualities are a part of that mental growth that makes you beautiful. Today, I have grown in certain areas of my life but I still have a long way to go and writing is my therapy. There are many days where I have heard negative comments about my appearance, from the workplace to grocery shopping, or simply going anywhere. The big headed, retarded, weird looking, cockeyed, ugly, slow, and negative comments became the norm of what I was used to hearing in my everyday life.

From past coworkers to strangers, those words hurt. There were many other negative comments I heard about myself from coworkers that I let get under my skin to the point where I eventually quit a job that I really needed to keep. There was another time I was a camp counselor, I remember one of my six-year-old campers asking

me why I had so many bumps on my face. I later thought to myself if people only knew the real scars are so much deeper
than acne scars.

    I used to think to myself I have to toughen up and just continue to ignore negative words. Sadly, instead of reporting an issue or seeking help, I would continue to just give up or quit these jobs. As I got older I learned to ignore and silence those negative voices. Even if you disagree with my definition of beauty, define beauty for yourself and what it means to be confident. Redefine whatever you see yourself as, just make sure it is positive. The physical attributes of young and aged beauty are both beautiful, because true beauty is from within. I am writing these words very repetitively so that my definition of beauty changes the way you think about the concept of beauty.

I am trying to go above and beyond with my definition of beauty for women and girls. When girls enter womanhood, it is a beautiful and sacred concept of her new-found growth. Our cultural differences separate the practices of how, where, when, and whom enters womanhood. I think being smart, responsible, and having an altruistic mind set are some of the characteristics of womanhood, besides the obvious physical traits that make us women. If you are a female that is different, beating the odds, and being a true leader within your community, or simply giving back with your skills, that makes you so much more beautiful than following the negative popular trends of the world. Standing up for what is right or dressing how you want does not make you weird or inadequate. As women, we are to set examples for younger girls, so they do not end up lost.

It is okay to wear makeup or show skin, but the amount of skin you show does not define your beauty nor worth, nor does the amount of makeup foundation. You do not have to give away all of your body in order to be beautiful. I encourage you to use your heart and mind to change the world, do not rely solely on your body to gain attention and praise. I often notice how women thrive off attention and use it as daily fuel. These women use their physical appearance to advance in certain fields of life. I only want to encourage more girls and women to use their minds instead of bodies to advance in life.

It seems as if the hyper sexual images of women and misogynistic media will never cease. However, I daily challenge myself to be optimistic in knowing that one day this will hopefully change and the female body will be respected. If your grandmother or mother gave you a special locket or bracelet, before they passed away, I am pretty sure you would value and take care of them. As opposed to just losing them or throwing them away in the trash. The way we value joy, peace, love, time, attention, forgiveness, honesty, and numerous other concepts in which money cannot buy.

We as girls and women need to value and highly regard our bodies as a sacred temple that cannot be purchased. I say this because our society promotes promiscuity as cool and some representations of womanhood and manhood are very false. To all girls and women, hold on to your true beauty, always being naked, or sleeping around may get you the popularity or cool card, but it is not worth the internal scarring that will forever remain. Your inner beauty represents your strength and innocence that many people will try and want to take from you. In your mind and heart you are beautiful warriors, so claim it! The world is full of negativity, so always wear your armor to protect your true beauty which is your mind, spirit, and heart. The armor is not makeup or designer materials, but so much more.

It is the ability to think and make decisions based upon wisdom, it is the ability to have self-control. It is the power and ability to say no as well as fight against the norm as women and girls. The armor is using the positive force within you to rid the world of negativity that tries to consume our lives. Beauty is not jealousy, envy, nor greed, it is the complete opposite. It is my social and moral responsibility that I challenge women and girls all over the world to redefine beauty.

Only you have the ability to change the way you view yourself, but I am offering an alternative to the physical definition of beauty. A woman's true beauty is often overshadowed by her physical attributes. We must value and praise the inner characteristics as opposed to only the physical and outer appearance. We live in a world in which we are teaching our girls to be narcissistic, selfish, and all the wrong concepts surrounding the definition of beauty. The judging of who's hot and who's not to beauty competitions, and judging the female body from head to toe. Think of these things as false, because we as girls and women are truly beautiful inside and out. The characteristics of true beauty are values with substance as opposed to the notion of "If you got it, flaunt it" mentality. There is so much emphasis placed upon a womans body image and physical appearance. To the point where girls and women suffer from eating disorders as they are dying to look thin. As opposed to the other cultures that praise a woman based upon a fuller body figure. There are so many issues we as women face and it would be great to eliminate body image as one of the forerunners. We will always have those days when "we just don't feel that pretty today." My goal is to inspire you as women and girls to have more beautiful days than feeling bad and ugly days. The days in which you wake up and look in the mirror and know you are truly beautiful.

This is when you wake up feeling and knowing your worth as a female and worth as a human being. Take at least one day out of the week to evaluate who you are and what makes you truly beautiful. Make a list of 5 physical and 5 nonphysical traits that make you beautiful. Discuss with a friend, mother, aunt, grandmother, or any female your answers. As women and girls we need to work together despite our differences. The next challenge would be to ask a female different from yourself (Age, religion, race, hair color, height, eye color, etc.) or female strangers 5 physical and nonphysical things that make them beautiful.

As you discuss and share your responses with one another, be open to making new female friends and understanding each of your unique qualities you all possess. These qualities are different but in similarity we are all beautiful girls and women. This is a short exercise in which it forces us out of our comfort zones in hopes of building healthy relationships, solidarity, and sparking conversations about our differences. While most of all uniting around those differences and realizing the beauty in diversity. By getting to know your partners name, and background through 10 concepts that make them beautiful. Overall take about 10 minutes to complete this exercise and another 10-15 minutes discussing, bonding, and collaborating.

If you have real qualities and interests in common, exchange numbers, emails, or whatever and challenge yourself to make a new lifelong friend, or as I discussed earlier a sister. At this point in my life now at 25 years old I have walked away from unhealthy relationships and God began showing me people and places to walk away from.

So, I am always open to bonding and making lifelong friendships with people that share similar values, beliefs, and overall interests to my own. From childhood through adulthood, make new sisters and build a healthy solid sisterhood.

My sister has always been my best friend and we make sure that our bond is kept tight, by learning each others likes and dislikes, as well as strengths and weaknesses. As we get older, we are pushing each other to be great, I learn how to be more confident from her, while I help her with organization skills. We are one others biggest critics, and supporters of each others dreams and goals. What can you help your fellow sister with, on her journey towards discovering her True Beauty? True Beauty is about taking the little steps to encourage your fellow sister. Take pride in your academic, social, and other accomplishments and skills that make you truly beautiful. Follow and pursue careers in which you are passionate about.

I plan to change the way we as girls and women view our bodies and the definition of beauty. As many of you reading this book may have felt ugly or inferior, or still feeling inadequate based on your appearance or abilities. Always remember to think of beauty as defined as something from within. That something from within is the beautiful light that not everyone can see until you show them. It is important that we as women radiate our beautiful light onto a world of darkness. Doing and saying nasty things do not reflect that inner beautiful light. To all girls, I say not only look beautiful, but be beautiful, by walking in beauty.

Unfortunately, I cannot change the way you all feel about what is beautiful and what is not. If you do not accept my definition of True beauty then challenge yourself to understand the real meaning of being beautiful. I also wrote this book because I do not like the destructive path I see girls and women heading down, the same path I was once on. I only encourage you all to stay on a straight path leading to success in life. Our girls are crying out for love, attention, and just for someone to listen and believe in them. So many times I wanted to give up on myself, but God always reassured me that I had to keep going. I will not give up on you so please as you read this do not ever give up!

    Whatever you do in life do not quit or give up. The potential and worth you obtain is so much more than what you may see in the mirror every day. The light inside of you is so beautiful and no one can see it until you allow it to shine. We all as women possess skills and talents that remain hidden until we truly discover and begin to tap into those skills. Once you realize your true beauty is not solely your physical appearance, then your true beauty, just like your talents and skills will be uncovered, and they can only be unleashed by you. For all of those people who doubt, hate, bully, or put you down.

To them I say silence their voices in your head, and let your beautiful light out shine their ignorance. I grew tired of letting everyone else's opinion define who Kara was, aren't you tired too? This change may not occur overnight for you, because it had taken me years. To this day I am learning to love the skin I am in and embrace my true beauty. Since I was 12 years old I let negative words from other people dictate my identity. I was used to rejecting myself, so that other peoples rejection would hurt less. I remember a time when I was in the 6th grade and sometimes I joked about my own hair and the size of my head, so that I beat my bullies to it, I rather insult myself and make them laugh.

I would rather quickly hurt myself, because the pain was easier to cope with, versus hurt from someone else. Once I discovered my true beauty and inner light, joy began to soon follow. Happiness is priceless in life and once you get a taste of it, it can be very addicting. As women and girls I challenge you to not let the past trials define your present nor future endeavors. I am pretty sure no female wants to spend their entire life in misery. It takes less energy just being happy, smiling and living out your true beauty. I ask that you remind yourself of your true inner beauty every time road blocks or ones ignorance is thrown your way.

If you ever get down, just remember that God created us in his perfect image and through his eyes we are all equally beautiful. The worlds definition of beauty is vain, unattainable, one dimensional, and excludes girls and women, like me and you. Wrinkles, acne, stretch marks, birth marks, scars, freckles, discoloration, gray hair, moles, and more are all symbols of beauty that God created you with. I'm begging and pleading that more women and girls embrace their natural features, in which they were born and have grown up with. There are people that get plenty of procedures done to change or enhance their beauty as it relates to their physical features.

However, some of these women are still unhappy and dissatisfied with not only their new appearance, but their entire life. Why spend so much money to change the way you look, when the true satisfaction from within may never come. All the millions and billions spent to alter the physical beauty, when the inner beauty can never be brought. The true beauty will result when you discover that inner light, I am coming to discover my own light through fasting, prayer, and constantly telling myself in my head that I am beautiful. Even when I hear negative comments from strangers and seeing past negative posts online, it is a daily challenge to keep my thoughts about myself positive.

Which is why I challenge you all to take a break from media and technology. The discovery of your true beauty is a process in finding out who you are as a girl or woman. What is your place in this world and how are you letting your beautiful light shine upon the world. I cannot re define beauty on my own, I need the help of millions of girls and women. Even if the definition of beauty does not change globally, it is still important to change and live by the alternative definition of inner beauty.

    I ask that you apply my words to your daily life as well as challenge the other girls and women in your life to be truly beautiful. As I have stated earlier that this task will not be easy, but re define beauty for yourself even if no one knows it. The beauty from within has to come from a place in which you have to dig deep in order to find it. Overall, I want (you) women and girls in this world to re define their position and existence in society. As I was coming to a conclusion I came to realize that in reality television women seem to dominate that arena. Almost all of the reality shows, we see women or girls not always behaving appropriately. However, the bad or inappropriate or controversial is what people see as entertainment and it is also what sells.

Overall, reality television is taking over and is becoming very influential amongst young girls. These same women we see cursing, bending over, throwing drinks, spitting on others, or fighting are praised as beautiful. In my first few years of undergrad, I would watch all of the female dominated reality shows. However, now I barely watch any of those shows and limit my intake, and as a young adult I began to think of ways to volunteer and somehow contribute to changing the world for the better. I started looking up mission trips internationally and thinking of ways to give back locally.

That is another reason towards the end of 2015 I created my bracelets Cherished Beautiful Creations based off my old blog. I started making fabric covered bangles with a positive message to give away and sale, in hopes of boosting girls and womens self-esteem. All of my creative pieces are a work in progress and by the grace of God I know everything will come together. I chose to use my words, books, and bracelets to give back. As well as donating my clothes and shoes to local shelters. How can you use your talent and skills to give back and uplift your fellow female sisters in this world? Instead of over indulging in the latest reality show and celebrity gossip, I also grew tired of watching wealthy people on television complain about miscellaneous problems.

Then I turn to the news, or read my CNN alerts and see that the world around me is suffering. These reality shows are obviously entertainment or conversation starters, but I hate the representation portrayed by some of the reality female stars. The ego, jealousy, greed, selfishness, are just some of the things that are portrayed within these shows. I think the fighting is always glorified and the image of successful or non-successful women never getting along is false. It is refreshing to see women being leaders, role models, mothers, entrepreneurs, and more using their platform responsibly.

With millions of viewers each week, it is always great to show women and girls working together, uniting instead of dividing. As women we must work together for the empowerment of all girls and women being beautiful. As well as being equally beautiful, so instead of tearing one anothers physical appearance down so much, let's try lifting one another up. We are all so divided around the world, yet if women and girls could just unite as beautiful, powerful human beings then this would be a great start to ending or at least halting this generational curse of mean girls and mean women in our society. This beautiful strong light from within could possibly help lead the world out of darkness.

All I ask is that you remember what TRUE beauty really is, even if you define it separately from my definition of inner beauty. True beauty is in your heart, spirit, and mind. True beauty is not only physical attributes, but it is the inner light inside of every single female and every human being. Always remember that you are precious and priceless and that you are capable of doing and accomplishing whatever you put your mind to. Do the work and continue to work extremely hard and I promise you that it will definitely pay off in the long run. I can only hope that you never settle for less or sell your body. The mind we have is so much more powerful than prostituting our bodies and assets to the 3 M's.

No matter how hard life gets, walk with grace, sophistication, confidence, and humbleness. In this life you do not have to ever become someone else or sacrifice your self-worth or dignity, in order for you to become successful and reach your goals and dreams. I just challenge you as girls and women to switch up your vocabulary, dress, but most of all for you to change your mind set about the definition of beauty. You can still look cute and be smart, as well as beautiful and sophisticated in your own way. As soon as you get ready to judge someone as something negative, just purge it out of your brain completely and try to at least get to know the person.

As we are taught when we are younger to not judge a book by its cover. I am on a mission to re define beauty with my definition of True Beauty, by embracing natural beauty from within and ending bullying. Body image and bullying are two issues that are close to home, as both have impacted my life and I can relate to many individuals who are/or is struggling with low self-esteem and bullying. Two of these issues are my story, and I grew tired of remaining silent. There are so many times when I'm praying and worshipping God for being such an awesome God and keeping me alive, when I know I should be dead.

All the times I traveled by greyhound bus meeting men by myself, I could have easily been snatched, raped, murdered, trafficked, but God kept me. To the time when I was in 6th and 7th grade and I cried so many nights, thinking about ways to kill myself with a protractor I had from math class and thinking if I take the pills I saw in the medicine cabinet would they kill me faster, but God kept me. No 11 or 12 year old child should be thinking about ways to kill themselves, no one period should ever consider suicide as an option. To the times when I allowed some of the men I met on the internet that were just "past times" do whatever they wanted to my body, God kept me.

I am still here and in one piece by the grace and mercy of Jesus Christ. I am not ashamed of the things I have done or said, because I learned from those mistakes. I did not know my worth or True Beauty, until God began working through me, therefore using his light to shine through me, and I thank God every day for keeping me. We all know the saying hurt people hurt people, well I was a hurt person hurting people and I allowed other hurt people to hurt me. Unfortunately, the vicious cycle continues in our society.

However, with my words in this book I plan to contribute to healing women and girls like myself that have suffered from always feeling ugly and being the target of bullying. Instead of hurt people hurt people, let's help hurt people heal, so healed people can heal people, no more hurting one another. We all have been hurt and now it is time to heal, which is another reason I named this chapter reborn beauty. Being reborn is a part of healing and starting fresh, which is why it starts with forgiving yourself and forgiving others. True beauty must be exemplified on all inner levels, the true inner beauty is what contains the substance of our beauty as women.

Always remember to never allow your age to define your beauty, that number does not define who you are, whether you or 8, 17, 36, or 72 years and older, you are beautiful, period point blank.
I refuse to allow the 3 M's to define my beauty and worth. I am so sick and tired of struggling with body image, should I eat to gain weight, or should I try to lose weight in order to look more like the models on television. So, you know what, I am going to enjoy my burger and milkshake, and if I

go work out tomorrow that is up to me and none of your business! So what if I gained or lost weight, as long as I am healthy that is all that matters! Heck my healthy may be a little different from your healthy.

I like coffee and a bagel with cream cheese, you may like a kale smoothie and protein bar. Some of us wear flats, heels, tennis shoes, or no shoes. We are all so very different and we must love and accept, as well as respect those beautiful differences. It is a constant daily battle in which I am so very fed up and exhausted of period. I am fighting back with my words and mind, because that is where all of the power lies. The body changes over time and so should our mindsets change and evolve. As I said earlier, I challenge you all as girls and women to be more leaders, educators, writers, doctors, inventors, lawyers, CEO's, surgeons, artists, journalist, engineers, dancers, cosmetologists, and the list continues. No matter what age, you can let your True Beauty shine.

As I have stated earlier the journey to finding your true beauty will not be easy, but you must start with telling yourself that you are beautiful daily. Just as you would praise a child for his or her accomplishments, you must remind yourself that you are beautiful and proud of yourself. It helps me when I tell myself in the mirror, "I am proud of you Kara and you are beautiful," this is not about anyone else but you, so practice saying that aloud. Whatever your passion and talent is, hold on to it tightly and never let it go, pursue it wholeheartedly, while not allowing it to be your sole identity title.

My main point is to let the true inner beauty shine without exploiting your precious and priceless gifts. In conclusion, be so much more than a pretty face that obtains no inner substance, you are worth so much more than a billion "likes, retweets, or shares." Stop worrying about breaking the internet with naked photos or twerking competitions, and decide today that you will stay focused. Stay focused on pursuing your passion with pride and dignity. Women and girls, walk in pride of your accomplishments, goals, and dreams. As I finally finish this book at 25 years old, I am walking slowly in my True Beauty. As I said before I have my days where I just feel kinda ugly, but I thank God I have been having more days of feeling beautiful and worthy.

The journey to discovering your true beauty will be a process, but you can do it. As a part of becoming a reborn beauty, your mind, heart, and spirit must be renewed and it starts with changing your thinking. I have been transparent about my anxiety, depression, low self-esteem, anger, suicidal thoughts and plans. Those thoughts started during 6th and 7th grade, when I no longer could take being bullied, I thought of many ways to kill myself, that also continued throughout college.

I addressed many different mental health issues I faced within this book, and in order for you to heal and move forward you must get help. There is nothing wrong with talking to a counselor, therapist, pastor, life coach, or someone that is qualified and can really help you. I challenge you to get help today and allow God to heal you from the inside out. In order to walk in your True Beauty, the first step is healing and defining your worth and inner beauty, second step is forgiveness, and then apply the definition of true beauty to your life. Forgive anyone and everyone who ever called you ugly or made you feel less than, and forgive yourself, because you have no control over the past, know that you are beautiful. Once you discover your true beauty, you will be set free from that box I was living in for so long.

As a quick re-cap, the definition of True Beauty is everything I have covered in this book. True beauty is your mind, heart, spirit, and inner qualities that make you unique. True beauty is your character and worth as a female, your True Beauty is that inner light that you possess. Lastly never allow the 3 M's to validate or define your beauty and worth, enforce your dreams and goals to come true. For all the times people in this world will call you not so beautiful things, you must never get tired of hearing how beautiful and worthy you are.

Always remember do not be afraid to unveil the light of true beauty from within your heart, mind, and spirit. True Beauty is not confined in a boxed definition of beauty, True Beauty has no boundaries, and the only beauty that matters is completely inner.

Last quick exercise:

Step 1: Memorize Beautiful Who, Beautiful Me, Beautiful You!

Step 2: Grab a mirror, or look in the largest mirror and say out loud, Beautiful who, Beautiful me (pointing to yourself), Beautiful you (pointing to the mirror, which is you).

Step 3: Practice this with another female in your life or female stranger, you both say the slogan at the same time, while facing each other, you can choose to hold hands. Then look at each other and speak at the same time, Beautiful Who, Beautiful Me, Beautiful you, lastly hug and remind your fellow sister that she is beautiful on the inside and out!

Sources

Pageant history
http://www.pbs.org/wgbh/amex/missamarica/peopleevents/e_origins.html

Beauty definition, dictionary.com
http://www.dictionary.com/browse/beauty

Hue Documentary
http://www.sepiafilms.com/productions/completed/hue/hue.html

Dove study
http://www.dove.com/us/en/stories/about-dove/our-research.html

http://www.huffingtonpost.com/2011/05/17/satoshi-kanazawa-black-women-less-attractive_n_863327.html

Made in the USA
Monee, IL
14 January 2020